OUT OF TUNE

OUT OF TUNE

DAVID HELFGOTT AND
THE MYTH OF *SHINE*

MARGARET
HELFGOTT

WITH TOM GROSS

WARNER BOOKS

A Time Warner Company

Warner Books, Inc., 1271 Avenue of the Americas, New York NY 10020
Visit our Web site at http://warnerbooks.com

 A Time Warner Company

Printed in the United States of America
First Printing: April 1998
10 9 8 7 6 5 4 3 2 1

Library of Congress Cataloging-in-Publication Data

Helfgott, Margaret.
    Out of tune : David Helfgott and the myth of Shine / Margaret
    Helfgott with Tom Gross.
        p.   cm.
    Includes index.
    ISBN 0–446–52383–6
    1. Helfgott, David.   2. Pianists—Australia—Biography.
3. Mentally ill—Australia—Biography.   4. Shine (Motion picture)
I. Gross, Tom,   II. Title.
ML417.H3H47   1998
786.2'092
[B]—dc21   97–32316

Book design by Giorgetta Bell McRee

To my beloved father

Contents

Notes and Acknowledgments

Much of the first half of this book relates to events that occurred many years ago; naturally, when attempting to recount such events in detail, there is always the possibility of lapses of memory. But in the case of the story I have to tell, I believe I can say with confidence that it is a fully accurate and objective one. Not only am I fortunate in being blessed with an extremely clear memory, but my recollections have become more focused over recent months as *Shine's* worldwide success has caused me to think harder about my childhood years. In preparing this book I have also been able to reread the extensive diaries, notes, and letters that I have kept over the years, as well as to speak to many relatives and family friends.

As far as events in the period before I was born are concerned, most of the information comes from my parents. I have also taken the precaution of confirming things told to me by my father, who passed away in 1975, by speaking to family members and others who knew him well, such as his dear and loyal friends Dr. Jack Morris and Ivan Rostkier, his cousin Zelig Lewcowitz—and of course to my mother.

The information about Czestochowa in Poland comes from the Museum of the Diaspora in Tel Aviv, the Yad Vashem Holocaust Archives in Jerusalem, the *Encyclopaedia Judaica,* and from personal recollections of friends and relatives.

In regard to the chapter on mental illness, I would like to thank the World Schizophrenia Fellowship and the Australian Schizophrenia Foundation (to whom part of the proceeds of sales from this book are being donated).

Where I have cited lines from the film *Shine,* these have been checked for accuracy against the officially published screenplay of the film, by Jan Sardi and Scott Hicks.

Tom Gross and I are extremely grateful to the following for their invaluable help and assistance: Michael Fox, Ron Tira, Tania Hershman, Daniel Chalfen, Simona Fuma, Natasha Lehrer, Rachel Temkin, Cara Stern, Dror Izhar (Israel Film Institute), our agents Beth Elon and Deborah Harris, and Larry Kirshbaum and Colleen Kapklein at Warner Books. I would also like to thank all the Helfgott family, in particular my mother, and all the people who kindly agreed to be interviewed for this book. I would like to add a special word of thanks to my brother Leslie and his wife Marie, who undertook much of the Australian-based research, and to Dr. Albert Jacob for his wise counsel on both medical and musical matters.

Most of all, I owe an enormous debt of gratitude to Tom Gross for his patient and skillful assistance and hard work in helping me to write this book, and to my husband Dr. Allan Fisher who has been a tower of strength and support.

1

OSCAR NIGHT

The night of March 24, 1997, should have been one of the most exciting nights of my life. That was the night my brother David performed live at the Oscar ceremony; a moment of great pride for him and for the whole Helfgott family. Not only did he receive a standing ovation from the glittering array of celebrities gathered together for the 69th Annual Academy Awards, but a worldwide television audience of over a billion people saw him hailed as a living example of the triumph of the human spirit over adversity.

Here was David being embraced by Glenn Close. Here he was sharing the limelight with another special guest star, the former world heavyweight boxing champion Muhammad Ali. Here was my darling brother being applauded and feted by the world. This should have been an utterly joyous occasion, marking the crowning moment in David's remarkably topsy-turvy career as a concert pianist.

Instead, I was overcome by a great sadness that night. As I sat at home in Beersheva in southern Israel, I felt dismay and foreboding. I knew that my brother Leslie in Australia felt pain and anger and that my mother had been crying.

The reasons for our despair and for David's sudden fame were one and the same: *Shine,* the film that supposedly recounts the true story of my family, and, in particular, of David's relationship with his father, Peter Helfgott. We knew that David's playing that night, combined with the fact that *Shine* was among the Oscar winners, would mean that millions more would see this already-popular film—a film that is an unforgivable distortion of the truth.

This is not to say that we were not happy for David and the success he has achieved since the release of the film; but any pleasure we felt was all but drowned out by our concern for the memory of Peter Helfgott. For if David was the hero of the evening, my father was the villain. As film star Billy Crystal, the guest host for the Oscars that night, put it to the audience, *Shine* is about "a mean father who made his son practice at the piano until his fingers bled, and then declared 'my son is dead.'"

The film suggests that my brother's promising career was brought to an abrupt halt at the age of 22 by a mental breakdown largely induced by a brutal father—a father whose brutality may well have had something to do with the fact that he was a survivor of the Holocaust. But all this is very far from the truth, and the film is a terrible misrepresentation of a generous and decent man, who was both loving and much loved.

The real Peter Helfgott was proud and strong, tolerant and tender, full of insight and wisdom. His story is a remarkable one. He was a self-made man whose intellectual powers bordered on brilliance. He wished his children nothing but happiness, and hoped they would share the love of music that had done so much to enrich his own life. David and he had a wonderful rapport—both at the piano and in countless other ways.

But the impression received by millions of filmgoers was one of a tyrant—an impression reinforced by reviews in many of the world's leading publications that characterized my father as "cruel," "threatening," "violent," "slightly less lovable than Himmler," "Führerlike." And it did not stop there. The implications of *Shine* as a "true story" became the subject of constant discussion in the press and on television and radio throughout the world.

Reviewers made no distinction between the film version of Peter Helfgott and Peter Helfgott the real man. How could they? *Shine*'s director, Scott Hicks, knew this when he chose my father as a subject for his film, relying on information supplied by Gillian, David's new wife, who only met David eight years after my father's death. The situation was very different from other recent unflattering bio-pics such as *Surviving Picasso* and *JFK,* films also criticized for their historical inaccuracy. There are thousands of alternative sources of information about the lives of Pablo Picasso and John F. Kennedy; not so with my father, plucked from obscurity to be transformed into a beast. "I have suffered great personal distress and public humiliation as a result of the completely false and misleading depiction in *Shine* of my dear late husband," says my mother.

There were no beatings in our family. There was no dark and oppressive atmosphere in our house, no fearful glances every time my father entered the room. The house was not "like a concentration camp," as the character called Margaret who represents me says in the screenplay.* There was no emphasis in my home on winning at all costs. Far from ruining David's career, my father deserves credit for nurturing his talent and paving the way for his success.

In making what is called a bio-pic, a film director should be allowed a little artistic license if dramatic effect calls for it, and of course it may be necessary to fictionalize parts of a story in order to compress it into a two-hour movie. But the makers of *Shine* have deliberately distorted the truth beyond all reasonable limits, while allowing the film to be marketed as a true story. "*Shine* is an utterly extraordinary true story," proclaimed full-page ads in the *New York Times* and other publications.

The film contains many travesties of the truth. My Polish-born father was not a Holocaust survivor, despite the film's use of barbed wire, burning books, and marks on his forearm to imply that he was. He lived in Australia from 1933 onward, arriving there six

---

*This line was cut from the film at the last minute but remains in the officially published screenplay that went on sale in bookstores after the film's release, has been reprinted four times, and remains on sale.

years before the outbreak of World War II. Nor was his accent German: he had never been to Germany in his life. Nor did he sever contact with David—the two remained close while David was in London. David was in fact living with my father again in Perth at the time of Peter's death in December 1975.

While suggesting that my father's harsh behavior drove his son to insanity, the film conveniently neglects to mention that there is a history of mental illness in the Helfgott family. My father's own sister was institutionalized, and this was almost certainly linked to the illness that my brother later developed. David did not collapse after playing Rachmaninoff's Third Piano Concerto in London in 1969, which he had in any case performed many times before—in Perth and Melbourne in 1964, for example.

The film also omits David's first marriage in 1971, to Claire*, a Hungarian Jew who survived Dachau concentration camp. Claire was shocked by the film's portrayal of her former father-in-law. She told me: "I have only one word for what they have done to Peter Helfgott. It's disgusting." Referring to the portrayal of Peter she said, "The film brings back to me my childhood memories when innocent Jews were accused of all sorts of things they never did."

Other "key players" in the film and in David's life, such as our former piano teacher, Frank Arndt, on whom the fictional character of Mr. Rosen is based, and Professor Sir Frank Callaway, who organized David's studies at the Royal College of Music in

*I have agreed with Claire that we shall not publish her surname.

London, are equally upset at the film's depiction of my father.

During the ten years in which Scott Hicks was planning and shooting the film, I made repeated requests to see the script, since I had heard that my family was intimately involved, and that I myself would be portrayed. But I was never allowed to see a copy. Nor was my mother. Hicks mainly collaborated with David's new wife, Gillian, who never met my father.

My concern is not only for my father's memory but also for my brother, who has been catapulted into stardom despite his still-fragile mental state. After only a few concerts into his grueling 1997 world concert tour, critics were already dubbing him "a freak show" and his performances frequently elicited savage reviews. Only time will tell what the long-term consequences for his health will be.

As I sat there last March, wondering why a film that contains so many false scenes and false ideas should be considered worthy of an Oscar, I decided I would try to right some of the wrongs. This book is not the plea of a devoted daughter desperate to defend her father at all costs, but an attempt to present the real story behind a film that cynically distorted the truth for marketing purposes. I hope to repair the damage that has been done to the Helfgott family by recounting the truth about my brother, his father, and our family.

2

MY DEAR FATHER, PETER HELFGOTT

To understand where David comes from, it is necessary to know a little about my father, a key figure both in David's life and in *Shine*. Pinchas Elias Helfgott—who later anglicized his name to Peter—was born in 1903 in Kamyk, a small town in Poland that was famous for making matzo, the unleavened bread that the Jewish people eat each year at Passover. Kamyk is located not far from a larger town where my mother grew up, called Czestochowa, which lies about 125 miles southwest of Warsaw.

My mother, Rachel Granek, who is known as Rae, was born in 1920 in another little nearby town, Klubutzka, but moved with her family to Czestochowa when she was seven. Her mother, Chaya, died when Rae was two, leaving her father Mordechai to look after her and her brother Morry. Eventually Mordechai married Chaya's sister, Bronia, and they had three more children—two girls, Gutka and Henya (both of whom were to die in Treblinka), and a son, Johnny.

Like many towns in Poland before the Holocaust decimated Polish Jewry, Czestochowa had a sizable Jewish population, and by 1900, 30 percent of the 40,000 residents were Jews. Czestochowa is known internationally as the city of the Jasna Gora Madonna—the Black Madonna—Poland's holiest icon. Because of this, Catholics from all over Poland traditionally made a pilgrimage to the city, particularly around Easter time. Unfortunately, many of them took part in anti-Semitic attacks on the local Jewish population. My mother has often told me of her experiences when she was out in the town with her friends, on a trip to the movie theater, for example. Anti-Semitic Catholics would shout abuse and hurl stones and all sorts of objects at them and other Jewish residents.

As was common among Jewish families in eastern Europe at that time, my father's family was fairly large. There were seven children in all: Miriam, Zelig, Na'acha, my father Peter; and then after Peter came Rivka, Abraham, and Hannah. Hannah, regrettably, suffered from a hereditary mental illness almost certainly associated with the one that my brother David later developed.

The Helfgotts were a very religious household, against which my father rebelled. They were ultra-Orthodox Hassidic Jews, who worked as leather merchants but also spent a great deal of time praying. Peter was a very forward-looking thinker, interested in technology and progress, and not very happy with his restrictive family environment. He believed in the notion that equality and the betterment of mankind could be achieved through socialism, which at that time was a very common view, and was shared by many world-famous figures such as George Bernard Shaw, Albert Einstein, and Charlie Chaplin. Personally I don't think they fully took into account man's nature, which doesn't always allow for such an altruistic way of life; but my father nevertheless retained much of his early revolutionary outlook for the rest of his life.

Peter not only longed to see a better world, he also wanted literally to see the world, and he ran away from home three times. The first time, when he was only about twelve years old, he was caught and brought back. But eventually, at fourteen, he succeeded in running away for good.

As World War I drew to a close and revolution stirred in Russia, it was a tumultuous period for a young teenage boy to be wandering around eastern Europe, and perhaps not surprisingly he made his escape by joining the navy, although he never talked much about this. An old cousin of my father's here in Israel, Zelig Lewcowitz, told me that as far as he knew Peter had probably enlisted in the British Merchant Navy. And this was something quite unheard of for a young Jewish boy from a small *shtetl* to have done in those days.

The term *shtetl* is a diminutive for the Yiddish word "shtot," meaning "town." Kamyk was a *shtetl* similar to those depicted in the novels of Isaac Bashevis Singer, the paintings of Marc Chagall, and films such as *Fiddler on the Roof* and *Yentl*. Life in the *shtetl* was very much based on a sense of community, with a warm and intimate lifestyle centered around the synagogue, the home, and the marketplace. Everyone tended to conform to common values. For my father to have run away and broken free shows that he was very strong-minded in those days, as he was later on, too.

In 1926, after his stint in the navy, my father moved to Palestine, where he stayed for nearly a year. He looked for work but at that time there was a great depression there, and he failed to find steady employment. Not having much money also made it hard for him to leave the country, a problem he eventually solved by joining a traveling circus as a circus hand. My father used to tell me stories about his circus life. For example, how he had nearly been crushed by an elephant that had pinned him into a corner. If a tamer hadn't happened to walk by and pull the elephant away, I wouldn't be here writing to tell the tale.

He also used to show me the scar on his hand that he had received from a playful tiger. There is a scene in *Shine* where he shows the scar to my sister Suzie; but the director chose to move the scar from my father's hand to his forearm—and not to identify clearly what it was. In my opinion this was done deliberately, leaving the audience to assume that this mark was a concentration camp tattoo and that Peter was a concentration camp survivor, which was not the case. They are helped to arrive at this conclusion by the film's dialogue: almost immediately after revealing the mark on his forearm, Peter says, "No one can hurt me! Because in this world only the fit survive. The weak get crushed like insects." Certainly several film critics describe Peter Helfgott as "a concentration camp survivor" in their newspaper reviews, no doubt as a result of this and other scenes in the film—for example, the one where David says, "Like Daddy and his family before they were concentrated" (scene 18 of Scott Hicks and Jan Sardi's officially published screenplay). This is a subject I shall discuss more fully in Chapter 17.

After leaving Palestine, my father ended up rejoining the navy. In the early 1930s this took him to Australia, where he decided to settle, becoming a naturalized Australian citizen in 1936 at the age of thirty-three. Before that my father had paid one more brief visit to Poland; he missed his family, particularly his mother, whom he still cared deeply about in spite of having run away.

Once in Australia, he went to Melbourne, a place where many of the Jews from Czestochowa and nearby towns went to in those days. What usually happened was that someone from a particular town, often when fleeing pogroms, arrived in a certain city and then wrote to his friends and relatives to come out and join him there. Thus many Polish Jews bound for Australia ended up in Melbourne while Jews from Hungary, for example, tended to go to Sydney. The Jews would build up a *landsmanschaft,* an informal organization for Jewish people who came from the same town in Poland. Self-help has long been a very strong trait of the Jewish people: with the huddled, supersupportive communalism of the Diaspora, one could say the *shtetl* was the epitome of self-help, and these traditions were continued in Melbourne and Perth.

By the time my father arrived, the Jewish community in Melbourne was already well established, having been officially created in 1841, which was only six years after the foundation of Melbourne itself. In fact, two of the fifteen members of the Port Phillip Association who founded Melbourne in 1835 were Jewish, and since then Jews have done extremely well there. Indeed, the city's two most honored citizens, Sir John Monash and Sir Isaac Isaacs, were both Jewish. When Monash (who commanded the Australian and New Zealand forces during World War I) died in 1931, tens of thousands of people lined the route of his state funeral procession in what was one of the biggest funerals Australia has ever witnessed. Sir Isaac Isaacs—the son of a Polish-born tailor who went on to become Australia's first native-born governor-general—also received a state funeral. There were several other prominent Jews. For example, Edward Cohen was mayor of Melbourne in the 1860s, and Sir Benjamin Benjamin was mayor in the 1880s.

On arriving in Melbourne, my father lived in a little cottage in Pigdon Street in an area called Carlton, near the center of the city. Carlton used to be a poor working-class district full of Jewish refugee families, but today it has become a fashionable neighborhood, filled with designer boutiques, spaghetti bars, and ice cream shops. Peter tried his hand at a number of trades. He started a clothing company called Original Suits and he opened a tailoring factory, primarily for the manufacture of ladies' clothing, in a little lane at the top of Bourke Street in the center of Melbourne. My father would cut, design, sew, and make up garments, as well as deal with all the mechanical aspects of the machinery. (It was very common for Melbourne Jews, particularly at that time, to work in the garment industry.)

By nature my father was a very creative and enthusiastic person, always thinking up new schemes. Among other things, he invented a pressing machine for ironing clothes. The machine was designed to lift up the very heavy irons and presses used in tailoring factories, thus taking the weight off the person operating the iron. My father's machine was fairly successful and he sold at least twenty. He also invented a special kind of boiler.

He tried his hand at a number of inventions, but he didn't make much money from them. He also had several partnerships over the years, but his businesses were usually failures. As his good friend Ivan Rostkier recalls, his trusting personality meant that even though some of the businesses went well, his ideas were often copied by others and he was taken advantage of.

Although it was reasonably successful at first and he employed twelve people there, his clothing factory eventually went bankrupt. My father, who was very good at adapting to changing circumstances, then turned the premises into a coffee lounge. A self-taught musician, he used to entertain the customers in the evenings by playing the violin and piano and sometimes also singing. The place was apparently very successful and people have often talked to me about its enjoyable atmosphere and lively ambience. "It was the hot spot of Jewish immigrant life in Melbourne," one of my father's old friends told me. It was also of great significance because it is there where he met my mother in 1939.

My mother, Rae, was the eldest of five children. She was born in 1920, her brother Morry was born in 1922, her half-brother Johnny in 1924, and her two younger half-sisters Gutka and Henya in 1926 and 1928. My mother's father, Mordechai, was a very poor tailor. The whole family lived in a three-room flat in Czestochowa and Morry and Johnny had to sleep together in a box. In the daytime, Mordechai would close up the box and convert it into a work top for cutting coats and doing his tailoring work. My mother shared a small bed with her little sister Gutka.

After the widespread pogroms in Poland in 1936, and with Hitler intensifying both his expansionist and his anti-Semitic policies, Mordechai was desperate to flee Europe. He decided the family should move to Australia, where a brother of his had already settled and could secure them visas. But my grandfather didn't have enough money to buy tickets for everyone, so it was decided that he should travel first with the older children, and that Rae's stepmother Bronia and the three younger siblings would follow them a short while later.

My mother, Mordechai, and Morry bade an emotional farewell to the rest of the family, confident they would soon be reunited in Australia. But with the outbreak of war the other half of the family became trapped. It was not until 1946 that Bronia (having survived Bergen-Belsen) and Johnny (who survived Buchenwald) were finally to make it to Australia. The two youngest girls, Gutka and Henya, were gassed to death in Treblinka.

But my mother sailed from a port near Gdansk on the Baltic Sea on November 6, 1938, and arrived in Melbourne seven weeks later, on Christmas Day.

It was at his coffee lounge one evening when my mother went to go dancing that she first met my father. Dances were often held there in the evening, when the place changed from a serene central European-style coffeehouse to a boisterous dance hall. My mother loved to dance, especially to the kind of music that was popular at the time: waltzes such as Strauss's "The Blue Danube," big band music such as Glenn Miller's "In the Mood" and "Moonlight Serenade," or the swinging sounds of Benny Goodman. My mother says that the dances held at my father's coffee lounge were grand affairs, with the upbeat music and lively crowds mingling to produce a superb atmosphere.

When Peter saw Rae, who was seventeen years his junior, he fell for her at first sight, an attraction and love that was to remain steadfast for the rest of his life. My mother, then eighteen, was exceptionally pretty, with dark wavy hair and brown eyes. Peter was short and stocky. He had a round face and wore glasses, which were often perched on top of his head; he had thick curly hair (similar to David's) that was to thin out over the years, and clear intelligent blue eyes that were completely lacking in guile. He was of pleasant appearance, though not especially handsome. My mother tells me she found him good-looking, and was dazzled by his charm and fascinating conversation, and was happy to accept his invitation to dance.

My father courted her assiduously for five years, of which they went out for three, until they got married in 1944. According to my mother, my father had a few girlfriends before he met her, and she had been out with a few boys, too, but once they met they had eyes only for each other.

"I had other proposals of marriage," my mother told my brother Leslie and me recently, "but I wanted to marry only him, and he wanted to marry only me. He was helpful and considerate, whether in carrying my bags, taking me shopping, buying me flowers, or going out and buying me oranges and squeezing fresh juice for me. He was very solicitous and used to treat me like a queen."

About their marriage she said, "Peter was a very good husband. More than this he was also a good friend. When I met him I was actually pretty run down, worried day and night about my family in Poland, and working extremely hard to save money to bring them out to safety. Peter would comfort me; he was so tender and reassuring. He used to call me his little 'Pupechka' [a word derived from Polish, meaning 'doll']. He was like a rock of stability and loyalty to me. And he remained so throughout the rest of his life."

Initially my mother's father thought Peter might be a bit too old for her but in the end he gave his permission for them to get married. The wedding, in the Carlton Orthodox synagogue in April 1944, was small, with about thirty guests, and was followed by a reception in a nearby hall. "It was the happiest day of my life—the only sad note was the absence of our missing families in Europe," my father told me many years later. After more than a quarter century of wandering, Pinchas Elias Helfgott had finally found a wife he loved and was ready to start a new life with a family of his own.

3

FAMILY LIFE

I was born in March 1945, the eldest of five children. Next came David, born two years and two months later in May 1947. Leslie arrived in 1951, Suzie in 1953, and Louise, who is fourteen years my junior, in 1959. Unlike elder children in some families, who can be jealous of younger arrivals, we were all very excited and thrilled about each new addition to the family. The atmosphere in our house was warm and vital and we all got on well with one another. David and I in particular were very close and did many things together from an early age.

In accordance with Jewish custom, David was named after my father's father and I was named after my father's mother, Malka, which means "queen" in Hebrew. However, growing up in Australia, it was thought best to anglicize my name, so I became Margaret, which is actually on my birth certificate although Malka remains my Hebrew name. My second name, Chaya, is that of my maternal grandmother and is also Hebrew. It means "life." David is both my brother's Hebrew and English name, and he wasn't given a middle name.

Some of my earliest memories, from when I was about three years old, are of my father singing me lullabies as he gently rocked me to sleep. His and my favorite was "Ma Curly-Headed Babby," which is a wonderful old African-American plantation song. My father would take me on his knees and hold me in his arms and sing me its sweet-sounding words and melody. He seemed to know instinctively how to put a young child to sleep with the sounds of the music.

Although my father had left school at fourteen when he ran away from Poland, he had a great respect for education. He was an autodidact—most of the knowledge that he acquired was through his own interest and motivation—and he read a great deal. His native languages were first Yiddish and then Polish, and he had taught himself to read and write in English in his twenties. He loved reading books on physics, astronomy, nature, and so on. He encouraged all of his children to read, not only factual books but great literature, too—French writers such as Rolland, Zola, and Flaubert and Russian novelists such as Tolstoy, Chekhov, and Dostoyevsky. The love of reading that my father instilled in me as a child has continued to this day, and I still read at least one novel every week, as well as much nonfiction.

The extent of my father's self-education was remarkable. He came from a background that was in many ways unworldly. Until he ran away he had been to a *heder,* a Jewish religious school at which practically no secular studies were taught. His own father's reading was mainly limited to the Torah (the five books of Moses) and the Talmud (the collection of writings constituting Jewish civil and religious laws). Yet Peter was very intellectual, very musical; he was creative, an inventor, a passionate lover of life, and an idealist. At the same time, he was very conscious that he should help my mother with the cooking and shopping. He had felt uncomfortable as a child in Kamyk, where his father spent much of the day praying while his mother did all the housework.

He was always teaching us things, but in a very natural way. He used to point at the stars and tell us about astronomy. He told us which was the closest star, how many light-years away it was, what it was called. He explained how the atom is constructed and about molecules and protons and neutrons. And all this he taught us at a very young age, when I was about ten. He had a remarkable ability to explain even the most difficult and complicated scientific facts in a very clear and comprehensible way, and we would understand in an instant what he was talking about. We would sit around the kitchen table and he would draw us a chart on a piece of paper. Once I remember him cutting up a cake as a way of trying to explain how the atom could be split. "Isn't it incredible?" he would say, his eyes lighting up with awe as we sat there gripped. I tried to imagine just how minute these little particles that we couldn't even see were. I often wish that the teachers I had later had explained things as well as my father did when we were children.

He also taught us all to play chess. We would play with him or play among ourselves. These games were not only a lot of fun—we often held friendly family competitions—but I think that in many ways they actually prepared us for life. Chess always requires planning your next moves, charting out a course of action: life requires such forward-thinking, too. My father explained in a fascinating way what each piece could do, what powers they were invested with. These games—David and myself, Dad and David, Dad and myself, and so on—were an integral part of growing up in the Helfgott household.

My father's great love of life extended to animals and nature, too. He would buy David and me all sorts of books on animals, especially ones about the big cats (lions, tigers, leopards) and we all took a great deal of interest in the cat world. Our house was always home to many ordinary domestic cats. At one stage we had six, including a mother cat that had litters from time to time. As kids we spent a lot of time playing games with the kittens. David loved cats— they used to sit on top of the piano while he played—and as an adult, he named his cats after composers, Debussy and Rachmaninoff.

And of course, above all, Dad taught us music, which I shall discuss in Chapter 5.

My father also placed great stress on the importance of physical education. David in particular became very strong physically. He could walk up and down on his hands for about a half hour nonstop in the backyard. My father taught us how to do this and David's powers of balance were quite remarkable. Nowadays, David still does a lot of exercise; he goes swimming for lengthy periods almost every day and is very fit.

As children, we were constantly doing somersaults and exercises. Cartwheels were my favorite—I imagined I was a Russian acrobat. Later, in Perth, my father actually built a couple of parallel bars in the backyard. He used to whirl himself around them, even though he was over fifty—he had learned how to do this in the circus. Though we didn't manage that particular exercise, David and I were very conscious of keeping fit. As far as I'm aware, the habit of walking on the hands was unique to our household in Melbourne and also later in Perth. No doubt this helped David build up very strong hands for the piano.

We lived in a number of homes growing up, all of which were rented. It was in fact my brother Leslie who bought the first Helfgott home years later in Perth—my father contributed to the cost of Leslie's house but the bulk of it was paid by Leslie, who earned the money by traveling to the north of the state to work as an electrician, which paid very well.

In Melbourne, we lived in an apartment on Glenhuntly Road in an area called Elsternwick. The apartment had a big living room and a dining room connected by double glass doors, which my father removed in order to put up a swing. We had lots of fun taking it in turns to swing around at home.

I also have particularly fond memories of Friday nights during my childhood. Friday night was always party night. Even though he was a man of modest means, and often went through periods of financial hardship, my father would always arrive home from work on a Friday night with sweets, cakes, soft drinks, chocolates, and all sorts of goodies, and we had these wonderful parties. Dad wasn't a religious person—in fact quite the opposite—but he neverthe-less chose to hold the parties on Friday nights, when Jewish families would come together for a meal at home to celebrate the beginning of the Sabbath.

We were really quite poor growing up. For many years, we didn't even have sufficient gas or electricity for hot running water. I remember as a child we could have a bath only once a week and had to make do with a wash in cold water on other days. Having a bath was a big event and the whole procedure of preparing it took hours. We had to chop the wood in our backyard, stoke up a fire, wait for about an hour until the water got hot, and then fill up a bath. My fa-ther did most of the work but we helped with the chopping sometimes.

The first time we had hot water heated by gas was many years later when we moved to South Perth; it was like a miracle. Even now I regard hot water as something to be treasured: the luxury of just turning on a tap and having hot water gush out. On the other hand, chopping the wood was very good exercise and could be fun—except when the ax got stuck in the wood and my father had to come and pry it out.

Although we may not have had all the little luxu-ries that many other people take for granted growing up, our childhood was certainly never boring—there was music; there were political and philosophical dis-cussions; there were animals, astronomy, chess—al-ways something interesting and lively going on. The atmosphere at home could hardly have contrasted more completely with that depicted in *Shine*, where our house is portrayed as being very dark and oppressive. In the film, my father's entrances are often accompanied by ominous music and fearful glances. To describe my father as a "tyrant" or "brutal," as critics and journalists who know him only through the film have done, is a total travesty of the truth. To describe him as "slightly less lovable than Himmler" or speaking like the "führer" is quite absurd.

In fact we had a lot of freedom as children, so much so that David and I used to draw all over the walls of the lounge with crayons and pencils, making an absolute mess. But we were never told off for this. It didn't seem to worry my parents and they didn't mention it.

We would go out quite often. My father's mode of transportation was great fun, but rather hair-raising. He owned an old three-wheel motorbike with a big passenger compartment (a sort of large boxlike container) attached to the back in which all the family used to sit. Melbourne has a tram system and when we crossed the tram tracks, I sat in the back watching out for the trams, terrified that one would come along and knock us over. I was about eight at the time, David about six, and Leslie two, and I was always on guard for the family. Dad was a very skillful driver so although I was scared, I knew that nothing was going to happen to us.

Mom, Dad, David, and myself often went to the ice-skating rink in Melbourne. We had great fun whizzing around and occasionally falling over. David and I also loved going to the Saturday movie matinee. My parents would give us some pocket money to buy tickets and an ice cream, and I would take my little brother by the hand and we would trot off very happily to the movie theater every Saturday afternoon to see wonderful films such as *Francis the Talking Mule* and *Lassie Come Home.*

It was at about this time that David began going to school. In many ways, he was something of a late starter. He didn't actually begin talking until he was about three years old. He also had a lot of trouble controlling his bowels when he started school, at the age of five. He often hid in the grass after class near our school (Elwood State School, which was a few minutes' walk from Glenhuntly Road where we lived). I would leave school with my friends, and one of them would say, "Look, there's your little brother hiding in the grass." I would go over and fetch David, who had dirtied himself, and take him home where my mother would put him in a bath to clean him. David did this frequently, almost every day. To me, this kind of behavior illustrates what a sensitive and anxious child he was.

David messing himself was just a fact of life, something we got used to. My father never whipped David for this with a wet towel as happens in *Shine.* He never hit David, nor would it have been in his nature to do so.

I also recall that David didn't much want to go to school: he cried frequently, not wishing to be separated from his parents. I remember, too, that as a young child he was also scared of lighting the gas kettle. Even when he was older, David was not very practical. For example, as a teenager he couldn't tie his own shoelaces. Perhaps this was a foretaste of later life when David went to London and it soon became apparent that it wasn't good for him to be away from a loving, nurturing environment, without anyone to take care of him. In London he had difficulty looking after himself, managing his finances and surviving on his own. His reluctance to leave the family nest as a child was in marked contrast to myself; I didn't have any problems about going to school. On the contrary, I have always been curious and eager to try out new things, in contrast to David at that time.

David had to wear eyeglasses from a very early age. I think he must have been five, perhaps even four and a half. He was, and is, extremely short-sighted, the only child in our family who began to wear glasses so young. His glasses are the kind known in Australia as Coke bottle lenses because they are so thick. Nowadays David sometimes wears contact lenses, although he finds that they cause irritation. He may have been encouraged by others to wear them for his concert performances, even though he is not very comfortable with them.

Like my younger brother Leslie, who could be a bit of an adventurer and get into all sorts of mischief, I, too, was quite a naughty child. David was more serious, spending much of his time from an early age sitting at the piano, lost in music. I remember I owned a skirt that I absolutely hated and my mother would try and make me wear it. Early one evening I snuck out of the apartment and went down to the canal near our home in Glenhuntly Road and threw the skirt into the water and that was the end of that. That canal was perfect for throwing unwanted items into.

Another thing I remember is the circus that came to town every year. It pitched its tent on the big field just across from where we lived, bringing its horses and lions and tigers and elephants. I used to hang around day and night, intoxicated by the exotic atmosphere and nomadic feeling. David loved visiting the circus, too, and liked watching the firework displays that sometimes took place across the road from us, for example on Guy Fawkes night (an annual British tradition that used to also be celebrated in Australia).

I also had some rather macabre interests, and these got me into trouble. As a young child I was fascinated by matches and fire. When we stoked up the boiler I often used to throw an empty container of toothpaste into the fire, causing some chemical process whereby wonderful colors would be emitted from the old toothpaste container as it burned.

One day when I was about six or seven, I was in the kitchen standing near the very flimsy muslin curtains above the kitchen window. I was lighting one match after another seeing how fast they could burn down until they got to my fingers and then I would blow them out. Then disaster struck. I had stood too close to the curtains and suddenly they were engulfed in flames. I was alone in the kitchen and didn't know what to do. So I rushed to fill an empty milk bottle full of water and, like an idiot, threw it at the window—not realizing of course that the bottle would completely shatter the window. So not only was there now a fire burning out of control but there was also broken glass all over the floor.

Just at that moment, my little brother David came in and looked at the huge fire blazing and me stand-

ing there in a state of near paralysis not knowing
what to do. Shocked, he screamed "What have you
done! I'm going to go and tell on you." I was really
afraid I was going to get into trouble and I pleaded
with him not to. I had this vision that the fire could
be put out without anybody knowing, even though in
the meantime the wooden window frame had started
burning and I didn't know what to do. But David ran
off in a panic to tell my mother. Just then I noticed
my father's old gray shaving mug. I grabbed it and
began rushing back and forth from the tap, repeatedly filling it up and throwing water on the fire until
eventually I managed to put it out.

Now, although I was quite proud of myself for
putting out the fire, the kitchen still looked an absolute shambles. The curtains had been reduced to a
smoldering burned rag, the window frame had turned
completely black, and there were hundreds of bits of
broken glass from the window scattered all over the
floor amidst puddles of water. At that moment my
mother and David walked in, my mother looking horrified. Dad was due home from work shortly and I
was scared that I would be punished for all the damage I'd caused. So I hid in the bathroom. My mother
of course told my father what had happened. Dad
came to the door of the bathroom and said: "Come
on, Margaret, come on outside." And I said: "No, no,
no. I know I've done an awful thing. I don't want to
be punished." It took my father quite a long time
while I stayed barricaded in the bathroom to persuade me that nothing was going to happen to me.

Eventually I agreed to come out, and just as Dad
had promised, I didn't get punished at all. He simply

explained to me why it was dangerous to play with matches, and that was the end of it.

There was another incident a few months later where I again did something terribly stupid that could have ended in disaster. One of the things I used to be very curious about was the idea of hanging. I'd heard and read about people getting hanged for crimes, so I thought I would try to see what this hanging experience felt like. I suggested to David that we should try it out. Being my obedient little brother he did what his big sister told him. We went to the back of the apartments with a rope (our apartment was part of a small two-story block of four apartments, with stairs between the floors) and I told David to go up to the top of the landing while I stood at the bottom of the stairs. He then threw one end of the rope down to me as I instructed and I made a noose and put it around my neck. I then ordered him to start pulling. At first it was fine, but gradually I could feel the rope tightening around my neck and it stopped feeling fine. Luckily, just as I started gasping for air, one of the neighbors came out, saw us, and raced inside frantically shouting, "Mrs. Helfgott, Mrs. Helfgott, come quickly!" My mother rushed out, took the rope away from David, and I was saved.

4

THE MOVE TO PERTH

In 1953, when I was eight and David was six, my parents decided the family should move to Perth, which is on the west coast of Australia, facing the Indian Ocean and more than 2,000 miles by road from Melbourne. I once asked my father why, rather than move to say Sydney or Canberra, he chose to go to Perth, which is after all one of the most isolated cities in the world. (The nearest city, Adelaide, is over 1,700 miles away.) He told me that he'd taken out a map of Australia and picked the farthest place he could from Melbourne. Its distance was precisely the reason for the move. He wanted to make a totally fresh start.

When my father first came to Australia he had been reasonably successful. But over the years he suffered a string of business failures and things hadn't always gone well for him. (In 1942–43, he had served in the

Australian armed forces.) He also worked in a knit-wear factory, keeping the mechanical and electrical tools in order. But as well as disappointments with work, he had become disillusioned with several of his friends in Melbourne, which was particularly painful for him.

By nature, my father was a giver. He had a big personality with a big heart and would do anything for his friends. Yet several of the people he thought he could rely on had let him down badly. In the early days in Melbourne, he used to give shelter to newly arrived migrants from Poland—many of them refugees from anti-Semitic persecution—in his house in Pigdon Street. In most cases they had no money, and my father would feed, clothe, and look after them without taking a penny. He would find them jobs, and help them get established.

But many of the people whom my father had be-friended and helped failed to stand by him when he experienced tough times. This was the case even though some of them had become very wealthy. When my father had been in a position to help people, he had done so unstintingly; yet when he himself needed assistance, very little was forthcoming. I remember Dad telling me that people he had helped in the past, and who had since made a lot of money, had done everything they could to avoid him in his time of need. Even though he had four young children (Louise wasn't born yet), had lost his business, and was in financial difficulty, these people, when they saw my father coming down the street, would actually cross to the other side: they didn't want to have to place themselves in a situation where they might feel obliged to offer him help. My father was absolutely stunned by this behavior. When he used to tell me about these incidents I could see how hurt he was. My heart went out to him and I realized even then, at an early age, that people weren't always nice and didn't always do the right and decent thing.

There were of course two or three notable exceptions, with whom the family are still in touch. I recently spoke to Ida Zoltak, an elderly lady who still lives in Melbourne and whose husband David Zoltak had boarded with my father when he arrived from Czestochowa in 1937. She made a point of telling me that she had seen *Shine* and thought the way Peter was characterized was "a disgrace." "The real Peter Helfgott," she said, "was a very nice, gentle, and lovable man. I can only say nice things about him because there was nothing bad about him." Another person who became a lifelong friend after my father had put him up when he arrived from Poland in 1938 was Laizar Shaw. Laizar came to visit me in Israel a few years ago and also told me what a truly wonderful man my father was.

However, most of my father's so-called friends somehow disappeared when he needed them. This was one of the reasons why he wanted to make a fresh start in Perth, although the main factors were harsh economic conditions and his difficulty in finding suitable employment.

Before we sailed for Perth, Dad wanted to give David and me a special treat to put us in a good mood and prepare us for the trip. In June 1953, when Elizabeth II was crowned queen, all the kids in Melbourne were given a day off school to mark the event. Australia at that time was a very loyal member of the British Commonwealth. First Dad took us to lunch at a big department store in Melbourne called Myers and spoiled us with special kinds of candy and ice cream. Then we went to an amusement park called Luna Park. Its entrance was constructed so as to resemble an enormous clown's face and one had to walk through his giant wide-open mouth to get in. We had a great time there eating cotton candy and having a go on all kinds of rides; it was my first experience of the big dipper, which hurtled up and down at terrific speed and was so absolutely terrifying that I'll never forget it.

We made the 2,200 mile trip to Perth, which is the capital of Western Australia, by sea. Our journey took us first through Bass Strait (which separates the state of Victoria from the island of Tasmania) and then we sailed across the Great Australian Bight on the southern side of the continent. The boat took six days at that time, with no stops. All of us were utterly seasick, except for my father. We just wanted to stay in our cabin bed but Dad insisted that we go up on deck and breathe in the fresh air. After a couple of days of his urging, David and I finally emerged from our queasy slumber and went up on deck. The salty fresh air made us feel better in no time, and in the end the trip turned out to be quite fun. We ran around playing games all over the boat. However, the journey was an ordeal for my mother and father, since at the time Suzie was just a six-month-old baby and Leslie was only two and a half.

When we finally arrived in Perth, not only did we not have anywhere to stay, but we had almost no

money. Being broke, we first moved into an old factory warehouse full of gleaming white refrigerators.
The scene was really quite surreal. We all slept on
one big double mattress surrounded by fridges, and
we cooked on a radiator turned on its side. We lived
there for about three weeks until we finally managed
to find somewhere to rent.

During this time, although we had no house, no
furniture, nothing at all apart from food to eat, my father did something which, on the face of it, might
seem very peculiar. He decided to go out and buy the
family a piano. He did this on credit. It was a wonderful old second-hand Rönish piano, on which we
all learned to play. My brother Leslie in Perth still
owns it, indeed his young daughter Dorothy is learning to play on it. She's very talented musically, and is
continuing the family tradition.

My father had notified the Perth Jewish community
that we were moving to the town; the old system of
Jewish communal support was still very strong and
members were happy to help a new Jewish family
settle in. The Perth community, though small—at the
time it numbered about 3,000—was nevertheless a
well-established, vigorous, and affluent one. (It has
now grown to around 6,000, following an influx of
Jews from South Africa, Britain, and elsewhere.)
When some community members came to visit us in
the warehouse and saw that my father had purchased
a piano, they were absolutely astounded. "How can
you go out and buy a piano when you don't even
have a place to live for your children?" they asked. I
remember clearly that my father just looked them

straight in the eye and said, "But you can't live without a piano, you can't live without music."

That's what my father was like. His passion for
music and the vision he had of teaching us the piano
was fulfilled not only in David, but also to a lesser degree in myself and my other siblings. That we all absorbed such a great love of music was due to my
father.

But although music for him was as essential as
bread and water, he was not obsessive nor did he
lack a sense of proportion about what was important.
What he had was a spiritual side, a dream of enriching our lives, which paid as much attention to cultural
values as to material comfort. Buying us a piano
when he did was not a case of his being in any way
neglectful. We had plenty to eat during that period, as
we did at other times. In fact, my father was not only
a great believer in making us take sufficient physical
exercise, he was also a stickler for ensuring that we
always had the correct nutrition. He constantly made
a point of giving us the right quantities of protein,
fruit, vegetables, meat, and salads.

After moving out of the refrigerator warehouse, we
lived in a number of houses in and around a working-
class neighborhood in the northern part of Perth, called
Highgate. Highgate, which was populated by many new
immigrants, mainly from Italy, Greece, and Yugoslavia,
was next to a much wealthier area called Mt. Lawley,
where many of the better off, well-established Jews
lived. (Like Carlton in Melbourne, Highgate has in recent years become extremely chic, full of new bars and
boutiques.)

We first stayed for a few weeks at a boardinghouse

in Lake Street, and then for the next two years we rented a house in Beaufort Street. While we lived at the back of the house, my father decided to turn the front part, which was formerly a shop, into a European-style tearoom. We ran up pink curtains, decorated the tables, and made everything look as attractive as possible; but the venture wasn't very successful and after two or three months we had to abandon it. My father then went to work as an electrical fitter for the State Electricity Commission.

We were really quite poor. When we needed to economize further, we moved to a house we rented from the state housing commission in an area called Maniana. The house was cheaply constructed, made primarily of asbestos. Later we lived in a dilapidated house in another part of Beaufort Street, which is now a veterinary clinic. There were a lot of problems with the sewage there, and my father spent a great deal of time trying to fix it. The landlord just neglected the problem.

When we first lived in Perth we didn't have a fridge, which is rather ironic after being surrounded by them at the warehouse. To keep everything fresh, we had to buy an ice chest. In those days an ice delivery man would come down the street every few days, and the families in the neighborhood would buy a block of ice and put it in their chest along with perishables. Eventually my father had saved enough to buy a fridge.

Growing up in Perth, with its white sandy beaches and long summer days, was very different from growing up in Melbourne. They were two different worlds. Perth seemed much more informal to me. Maybe it was the more Mediterranean-like climate and the big open spaces that made life there seem to go at such a relaxed pace. Melbourne's weather is much cooler and more rainy, and above all changeable. Its inhabitants say of it that there can be four seasons in a single day. Perth had not only the beaches but the wide, tranquil Swan River, which cuts through the center of the city and is often dotted with yachts and sailing boats.

I had always worn shoes and socks in Melbourne, but in Perth a lot of people seemed to go around barefoot, and I quickly discarded my footwear when running around both at home and when playing with friends in the streets nearby.

Although Perth may be isolated, many people have heard of it. In the 1960s, its citizens burned their lights all night to guide the American astronaut John Glenn, who in 1962 became the first American to orbit the earth. The first thing Glenn saw when he entered the earth's stratosphere were the lights of Perth, and the city is still now known by many as the City of Lights.

It came to international prominence again in 1987 when it hosted the America's Cup—the first time the famous yachting trophy had been held outside the United States. Perth has also had its share of wealthy tycoons, such as Alan Bond, who in 1987 paid a then world record U.S. $53.9 million for Van Gogh's *Irises,* and Robert Holmes a Court, who in the 1980s was one of Australia's richest men.

The city's climate was truly tropical. Summer nights could be very hot, and sometimes we used to drag our mattresses out onto the back lawn and lie on our backs, looking up at the stars. And Dad would then treat us to an astronomy lesson. He had taught him-

self an impressive amount. He would explain the way
the galaxies were constructed. He would point up-
ward and show us the Milky Way, the Three Sisters,
the Southern Cross—everything that could be seen in
Australia's night skies.

The nearest star, Alpha Centauri, was four and a
half light-years away. My father would explain how
the light took off from it and how it would take four
and a half years to get to Perth. All this was fascinating for young children: David and I just absorbed it
all and asked lots of eager questions. These were our
science lessons, although we didn't even think of
them as lessons; it was just a natural part of growing
up. And where another family might talk about who
won the soccer game or what the neighbors were
doing, we would discuss the nearest star to earth, or
which ran faster, a leopard or a puma, or the best
move to make in a chess game when your king is
trapped between two bishops.

We regularly crossed to the south side of the city to
visit the zoo, one of our favorite places. We all loved
these outings, especially since my father was such a
great guide. He told us all about the animals, and
would conjure up wonderfully exotic memories from
his time in the circus.

We had a good life, even though we were relatively
poor. My father even bought me my first camera
when I was eleven years old. I loved it, and started
taking pictures of the whole family; most of the pictures of my father and David in this book are ones
that I took myself. There aren't many photos from
earlier years because no one in the family actually
owned a camera before that.

5

"MUSIC WILL ALWAYS BE YOUR FRIEND"

I asked my father one day why he had taught us all music and he replied: "If I had given you money and possessions, they could have been lost. But if I give you music, no matter where you are in the world, even if you are alone or without money, music will always be a friend to you."

His passion for music was tied to the notion that once you mastered it, it was yours, it was part of your being and no one could take it away from you. His love for music was, I believe, innate and not the result of some external factor or influence.

As with most of the things that he had learned, Peter Helfgott was a self-taught musician. He had mastered the piano while living in Melbourne, essentially by going to the houses of friends whose children were learning to play. He would sit with the child who was taking piano lessons and ask them to show him how they played, tell him the name of the notes, and so on. In this way, he learned both the piano and later the violin.

He was always drawn to music. He often used to play for us at home in the evenings. He would pick up the violin and play various Gypsy tunes—both joyous, invigorating ones and also melodies of the haunting, soulful kind, the product of centuries of persecution and rootlessness that the Gypsies have suffered in much the same way as the Jews. When in a different mood, my father would play the romantic Mendelssohn violin concerto, a melody from Tchaikovsky, or music such as "*Liebesfreud*" or "*Schön Rosmarin*," by the brilliant Vienna-born violinist and composer Fritz Kreisler.

At other times he would sit down at the piano and play something from the romantic period such as Liszt or Chopin, or a more popular piece such as "South of the Rio Grande" by Jacques Miller. It was remarkable how much he had taught himself, considering he had never taken a proper lesson in his life.

He told me that he would love to have become a musician but that the nature of his family in Poland had prevented him from fulfilling this dream. My father's longing for music dated back to his childhood in the *shtetl*. At that time he had even managed to scrape together enough money to buy a little violin. But when he brought it home, my grandfather, who intended my father to study to become a rabbi, was horrified. He took the violin and snapped it across his knees. This broke my father's heart and may well have contributed to his longing to run away.

Eventually, in Melbourne, my father did get to perform a little, entertaining the customers in his coffee lounge by playing the violin or piano and singing. But the fact that he was never able properly to fulfill his dream may have given him an added incentive to pass the gift of music on to his children. All of us play an instrument, and, at present, four of us are earning our living from music. Leslie plays the violin, performing in various ensembles as well as appearing as a soloist. He also teaches school children Australian bush dances together with other local folk dances. Louise has been teaching piano in the last few years. Perhaps more than any of us, she resembles our father in the sense that she is completely self-motivated and self-taught. She recently put herself successfully through both her theory and practical examinations without having had any formal training at all. Her pupils do exceptionally well. I myself teach piano and accompany various singers and instrumentalists. And of course, there is David.

Even Suzie, my one sister who doesn't actually earn her living from music (she's a social worker), obtained a music diploma from the Australian Music Examinations Board, which is a university-standard qualification.

There was other musical interest in the family, too. My father had a cousin who sang in a chorus in Czestochowa for two years and another who sold miniature musical instruments. According to Zelig Lewcowitz, my cousin in Tel Aviv, my father's father was also a very musical man, in spite of having broken Dad's violin. He would sing for hours on the Sabbath, which is a common practice in religious Jewish households. "David Helfgott loved to sing

Hassidic melodies," Zelig told me. "All the family used to go to David's sister Zelda on the Sabbath and gather round and listen to David sing. These were wonderful occasions. It was a way of life that has all but disappeared from eastern Europe."

Each night when we were children, my father would come home from work, have something to eat, and then sit with David and me and teach us to play the piano. The odd thing about David is that, though in the end he really did emerge as a child prodigy (he was undoubtedly a better pianist as a teenager than he is now), for the first two or three years of studying piano—until he was about eight—he totally failed to recognize the various notes that my father taught him. He was completely incapable of distinguishing one note from another. I used to think: Why can't he remember a C from a D or a G from an A? My father would say, for example, this is a G and it's on the second line of the treble clef, but the very next day David couldn't remember or began playing some other note. My father would patiently explain to him over and over again. "David," he would say, "that's a G, not an E or a B," and so on.

This went on almost every night for two years. It was as if my brother couldn't catch on at all. Then one night, to our complete surprise, after his previously almost unbelievable nonrecognition and noncomprehension of the music, David suddenly burst forth and found he could play the Polonaise in A-flat by Chopin, a very difficult piece that has two pages of octaves repeated in the middle section. As a pianist myself, I know how technically demanding this is even for an adult.

For a child of eight to play it so well was astonishing. I've never witnessed anything like it. It was as though David had started with no talent and gone on to win a medal at the Olympics. Even now in my work as a piano teacher, though I regularly see the way some children take an inordinate amount of time distinguishing notes whereas other children grasp them immediately, David's dramatic change in musical ability strikes me as exceptional. Having struggled in vain to learn even the most basic notation, David suddenly blossomed into playing difficult pieces superbly—it all seemed to fall into place. After that, he took off like a rocket; his hands performed brilliantly. As he put it some years later: "My fingers suddenly got hot."

Even before his breakthrough, when as a child of five or six in Melbourne my father first started to teach him, David had an absolute passion for the piano. During our time at primary school, we would come home fairly early and David would rush off to the piano and start tinkling away. Then at night he couldn't wait to be at the piano again for his lessons with my father. He certainly wasn't the kind of a child who had to be told, "Oh you must practice, and practice every day." I, on the other hand, had to be reminded to practice by my father and I was always making excuses about having other things to do. But David was completely in love with the piano from the minute he could touch the keys. He was both entranced and seduced by the sounds he could produce. The fact that he was having difficulty distinguishing the notation didn't make any difference; the love was already there.

After David's miraculous breakthrough, his passion

intensified. He was intoxicated by the music: you literally couldn't keep him away from the piano. The lessons with Dad were fun and not very serious—he wanted us, above all, to enjoy playing. David would discuss the music with my father, who would ask him questions or point out features in the music. Dad used to say that each note is like a diamond. "It's an important note, don't skip over it. It's like a gem, let it shine out." David and my father had a wonderful rapport at the piano.

That was the beginning of David's musical career. From then on he went from success to success. He could play virtually anything, however technically difficult. My father began to take us to small musical competitions. These were known in Perth by their Welsh term, *eisteddfods,* and were made up of different levels for different age groups. David and I would enter these competitions together, frequently as a duet. My father had built a long piano seat so that David and I could practice duets, and also so that my father and David could sit on the same seat and my father could guide David as he was learning.

David and I loved playing duets. Among our favorites were the "Jamaican Rumba" by Arthur Benjamin, "Schwanda the Bagpiper" (which comes from an opera by Prague-born composer Jaromir Weinberger, who based many of his melodies on Czech folk tunes), and classical duets by Mozart, Weber, and the German-born Danish pianist Friedrich Kuhlau. Obviously we aimed to do well, and I still possess some of the diplomas that we won, both playing separately and when we triumphed together.

But in general, they were gentle little affairs, where taking part was as important as winning.

Usually at the *eisteddfods* there would be a set piece for all the contestants in each particular level. For example, twenty eight-year-olds would each play the same set Minuet in G Major by Bach, which is a relatively simple piece. On other occasions, contestants were allowed to choose their own music. One such event, shortly after David's breakthrough, is portrayed in a scene near the beginning of *Shine*. David had entered the competition for nine-year-olds, which was not, of course, of a particularly high standard. But, to everyone's amazement, my brother went to the piano and played the Polonaise in A-flat. The packed hall went silent. You could have heard a pin drop. Nobody present could believe what they had heard.

The winner of this level was announced before the evening ended. David had undoubtedly performed best; he was head and shoulders above everybody else. But the judges said that it wouldn't be fair to the other children to give David the prize. "It would be like judging a primary school math class by the standard of Einstein," said one. They only wished to judge the children by a standard that was appropriate to that group. So even though they said that they were extraordinarily impressed with David, they gave the prize to someone else. In other words, David had been disqualified for being too good.

My father was absolutely flabbergasted by this reasoning, since David had won fair and square. He decided that it was time to leave. He took us by the hand, and we walked off home. It was not, however, as shown in this and other scenes in *Shine,* with my father deliberately walking ahead of David. Dad always walked with us. He never stomped off in front of us. He was annoyed not because he regarded winning as all-important, but because he felt upset for David, who had played so beautifully and was feeling upset and confused at having been deprived of the prize. I remember feeling just as David and my father did.

Later we received a letter telling us that at the end of that evening the judges had decided to create a special prize just for David and that he had been awarded one guinea, which was an enormous amount of money for an *eisteddfod.* (At that time Australia still used the old British currency and hadn't yet introduced Australian dollars.)

In the scene in *Shine* based on this *eisteddfod,* the actress playing my sister Suzie, seeing my father stomping angrily down the street, asks the actress who plays me: "Did he win or lose?" And I reply apprehensively: "He lost. Now we'll cop it." But in reality my father never stressed winning competitions, only doing one's best. As with virtually every other line attributed to "Margaret" in *Shine,* I certainly never said "we'll cop it" or anything of the kind.

My father taught us until I was about eleven and David was about nine. After David's breakthrough, my father felt he had taught us all he knew, and set about finding us a professional piano teacher. He read in a local Perth newspaper about Sue Tilley, a pianist who had received extensive training abroad and who had recently come back to Perth after working as a musician overseas. He rang her up and she suggested we come and see her. Having heard David and myself play, and been very impressed, she put us in touch with a music teacher friend of hers, Frank Arndt. When Frank heard us play, he was so excited by the standard we had reached for our ages that he agreed to take us on as pupils even though my father couldn't afford his fees. My father was extremely grateful to him for this.

So Frank became our main piano teacher, and he is the man on whom the character of Mr. Rosen in *Shine* is based. Except that in reality, far from Mr. Rosen suggesting we have professional piano lessons and my father being very reluctant to agree (as is depicted in *Shine*), it was my father himself who wanted us to have proper tuition and set about finding us a teacher. And at no stage was there the kind of animosity between my father and Frank as there was between my father's character and Mr. Rosen in the film.

David and I used to go together to Frank for our lessons. The first few times my father took us there, and then we went by bus on our own. Frank, who was then in his late twenties, lived with his parents in a large house near the University of Western Australia. He owned a beautiful maroon-colored Citroën car—it was a great treat when Frank took us for a drive in it. We felt like royalty. He also had a huge Labrador dog, which was bigger than I was and made me very nervous. David and I always held hands tightly when it bounded up to us as we went in the front door.

I remember the beautiful rosebushes and flowers in Frank's garden. By coincidence, the Arndt family gardener, Harry Millson, whom we used to see at the house, is now my mother's very good friend and companion in Perth. My mother and Harry met at a pensioners' social gathering, where they renewed their acquaintance. Their respective spouses both passed away some years ago, and Harry (at the ripe old age of eighty-nine) and my mother (who is seventy-seven) now regularly go out dancing and play bingo together.

We were taught by Frank for about four years. He was a great teacher, a wonderful person, and a marvelous musician. He deserves, together with my father, much of the credit for David's development as a pianist.

On a visit I made to Australia in 1996, after *Shine* had already been released there, Frank heard that I was in town and invited me to lunch. When we met it became clear that he did not just want to renew our acquaintance after so many years, but also to discuss *Shine,* which he said had dismayed him. He was extremely upset, he said, at the way in which Peter Helfgott was portrayed. "Your father was not like that at all," he reassured me, knowing that I had also been unhappy about the film. "He was one of the most gentle, nicest, and charming men I have ever come across." (No doubt fearing the strength of objections about the antagonistic relationship he had created between my father and David's music teacher, Scott Hicks changed Frank Arndt's name to Ben Rosen in the film.)

Under Frank's tutelage, David had made a lot of progress by the time he was twelve and he didn't seem to have any problem in learning difficult pieces. David was always practicing, so all his siblings would absorb the melodies of various concertos by constant exposure to them. I would hum a tune from one of them around the house as a matter of course, in the same way as a child today might sing something from MTV.

David used to perform at the Capitol Theater, which was then Perth's main concert venue and the seat of the West Australian Symphony Orchestra. (The Capitol has now been demolished and replaced by the Perth Concert Hall.) The whole family would go and hear him play and it was a thrilling experience for us all. We had to ensure David looked good and was properly dressed for such grand occasions, so any spare money would go toward clothes for him. My father had a lovely green corduroy jacket specially made up for him and he also wore smart trousers, nice shoes, and a cute little bow tie. David looked very elegant.

I felt very proud of my little brother up there playing with an orchestra. If it had been me performing in front of such a sizable audience at that age, I would have been very nervous; I used to keep my fingers crossed, hoping desperately that David didn't forget anything or make mistakes. But not only did he always get through the pieces without any problems, he played beautifully.

David soon began entering Australia's principal concerto and vocal music competition for young musicians, which was held every year under the auspices of the Australian Broadcasting Commission. First there were rounds in each state, then the winning pianist, instrumentalist, and singer would go forward to the nationwide final, known as the Commonwealth final, which was usually held in Sydney or Melbourne.

Every year David would enter this competition with a different piano concerto; he played concertos by Tchaikovsky, Ravel, Mozart, and Bach, interpreting their complexity quite brilliantly. He not only played them, he mastered them. He also played Rachmaninoff's Third Piano Concerto. He did not, as is strongly suggested in *Shine,* play Rachmaninoff's Third for the first time many years later in London, which supposedly led to his collapse. He had played it on a number of occasions, both publicly and privately, over a period of several years, before he even went to London.

All in all, David was creating quite a sensation with his musical excellence and was constantly being written about in newspaper reports. By the time he turned thirteen in May 1960, not a month seemed to go by without David receiving several rave reviews and write-ups.

"Head judge Dr. William Lovelock complimented thirteen-year-old pianist David Helfgott, who brought the most sympathetic applause with his dextrous handling of Ravel's often difficult Concerto in G Major," wrote the music critic Francis King in *The West Australian* on June 17, 1960.

"The audience was startled as thirteen-year-old David Helfgott gave an amazingly strong performance of the difficult Ravel Piano Concerto . . . David has that indefinable something—a quality which marks him for the future," wrote James Penberthy, the music critic for one of Perth's leading newspapers, the *Sunday Times*. "This is the first sight of a rare and prodigious talent, startling from one so young," he added.

"Individual talent was present in a highly promising young pianist, David Helfgott, who played three Hungarian dances by Brahms," said another review.

The music critic Sally Trethowan, writing in another newspaper under the heading "Youth Shines in Concert" (which may have provided the inspiration for the title of Scott Hicks's movie), said: "[Watching] the West Australian Symphony playing selections from Tchaikovsky's Sleeping Beauty ballet . . . in the State Final of the Concerto and Vocal Competition . . . Joseph Post, as spokesman for the three judges, said that the standard of piano playing was very high . . . and they had chosen David Helfgott as winner of the piano section."

These reviews of David's performances come from my father's collection of David's clippings, which he certainly never burned as is depicted in *Shine*. After he died Leslie kept the clippings, and then passed them on to David. I made myself some copies years later.

Naturally, after winning the annual State final to such acclaim, which he did on many occasions, David felt very special. There was always an air of anticipation in the house in the days before he prepared to be sent for the plane ride on the long journey to one of Australia's larger cities, Melbourne, Sydney, or Adelaide, where the Commonwealth Finals of the Concerto and Vocal Competition would take place. There, he would play with the resident ABC Orchestra. He would usually be accompanied by my mother or father, while the rest of us would gather around the radio at home, listening intently. Television only arrived in Australia in 1956 and we did not yet have a TV set. By the time David played in the concerto competition, because he had spent so many hours practicing them at home, we all knew those concertos by heart.

Surprisingly, given the fact that David really was an outstanding pianist at the time, he never actually won the Commonwealth Final. Nevertheless, every year was taken up with the excitement of these concerto competitions.

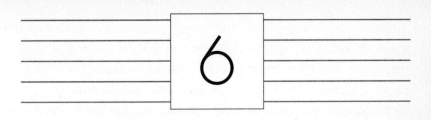

6

A SUGGESTION FROM ISAAC STERN

From the age of about twelve or thirteen, David's personality started to change. He was no longer the kind little boy that he had been. The previously sweet, introverted, and sensitive child became increasingly arrogant and selfish. Nowhere was this more obvious than in the realm of music, where he became very dominating and hated to share the limelight. He used to say: "There should only be one star in the family," leaving us in no doubt about whom he was talking.

Until then we had always played the piano happily side by side. But now when we sat down to practice together for competitions, David would start playing very loudly and very fast. Sometimes it was so loud that I couldn't even hear myself. When I asked David to play a little slower or a little softer so I could keep up with him, he would do precisely the opposite and pound away furiously at the keys.

This kind of uncooperative behavior continued until it became impossible to play with him. For me this was heartbreaking: I had always imagined that even though David was giving astonishing solo performances, we could still carry on performing together as a team.

I was not the only target of David's unpleasantness. When our little brother Leslie had first started to learn the violin, David often accompanied him on the piano. They really enjoyed playing together, and Leslie was especially delighted that his big brother was devoting time to him alone. But one day I remember listening with horror as David was accompanying Leslie, who was practicing. It sounded all wrong to me—out of time—which wasn't like David. I remember thinking: "Heavens, why is he playing like that? He's not supporting Leslie—he's playing too loud and too fast." Poor Leslie was only little and didn't seem to notice what was happening, but it wasn't long before it dawned on me: David was deliberately sabotaging Leslie's efforts.

My mother and father also suffered from David's odd behavior. When we went to the Concerto and Vocal competitions at the Capitol Theater, David started acting as if he no longer even wanted to know us. He walked ahead of my mother, father, and me as if he felt ashamed of us.

David even started behaving cruelly to his beloved animals. He had always loved playing with Bitzy, the good-natured neighborhood dog, who would often trot over to visit us. Then, suddenly, he took to kicking Bitzy—behavior that astonished us and made me feel terribly angry.

It is difficult to know whether David's strange behavior was merely an early sign of a difficult adolescence, or an indication that something more serious was afoot. My parents never talked to me about David's moods. Perhaps when they were alone they discussed their talented son. Maybe they simply concluded that geniuses are prone to difficult periods. I believe that David probably regarded all of us as competition and wanted to put us in our place so that he could be "the only star" in the house.

The way my parents spoiled David, in spite of his bad behavior, made growing up with him tough for the rest of us. As a reward for playing the piano so brilliantly he was always given one more lamb chop or an extra pint of milk. My father felt that David needed to be strong if he was to excel at playing the piano, and David had no problem obliging. He had such a voracious appetite that he could eat six lamb chops at a single meal.

Despite David's moods, the relationship between him and my father continued to be close. David was the apple of my father's eye, and my father did everything to encourage him. If there was any spare money, it was spent on nice new clothes for David. The rest of us couldn't help but be a little resentful of this special treatment, feeling that things should have been more equally shared.

My father's preoccupation with David was particularly hard on me, because I desperately wanted him to recognize my achievements too. I took my Junior Certificate examinations at the age of fifteen and passed all nine subjects, from art to commercial studies. This was an above-average performance in Perth and I proudly raced home to show everybody. When I rushed up to my father and told him that I had passed my Junior Certificate he said, "Shhh, David's practicing." That was the only reaction I got. The next day at school I found out that all the other children's parents had given them radios, clothes, and all sorts of presents for passing. But all I had received was a "Shhh, David's practicing."

I began to understand our situation better later in life. Books such as Carol Easton's biography of English cellist Jacqueline du Pré and a psychological study called *Nature's Gambit* by David Henry Feldman taught me how hard it can be for the other siblings to get enough attention when there is an exceptionally talented child in a family. It was especially so in our case, since we were all studying hard and learning musical instruments.

As he won praise on all sides, David's arrogance grew. One particular incident in the spring of 1961 had quite an effect on him. Shortly before David's fourteenth birthday in May, the American violinist Isaac Stern and the pianist Abbey Simon were on a tour of Australia. After hearing David perform at the West Australian State Final of the ABC Concerto and Vocal Competition, the two musicians were very impressed. They described David as highly talented and suggested that it might be a good idea for him to pursue his musical studies in the United States.

Stern and Simon were such celebrated personalities that their comments were taken up by the press and turned into feature stories. The music critic of the

Perth *Sunday Times,* James Penberthy, wrote a prominent front-page article. Under the heading "He'll Bring Honor to Perth," the paper announced it was setting up a fund for David to send him to America. Initially David was quite upset by this article because it revealed that he sat on a homemade stool, that he couldn't reach the pedals, and that his pant legs were too short. But he soon became very excited by all the media attention.

Many other papers followed the *Sunday Times'*s lead. Under the heading "Will He Be a Genius?" accompanied by a huge, half-page photo of my brother, a caption in one paper stated: "David Helfgott is already being hailed as a coming genius who could bring great credit to Australia. Two world-famous artists, Isaac Stern and Abbey Simon, have declared that David displays great promise and should go abroad to study."

Another paper reported Simon as saying, "David should go to one of the great schools of music such as the Curtis Institute in America"—a reference to the famous Philadelphia music school founded in 1924 by Mary Bok in memory of her father Cyrus Curtis. Simon, who had also been a child prodigy, had himself studied at the Curtis Institute.

An especially glowing article appeared in *Woman's Day* in July 1961. Entitled "Little Boy on Way to Fame," it began: "Children, housewives, old people on an evening stroll often pause a little awed, outside a modest home in Highgate, Perth. From the home tumbles a tempestuous stream of music played with an intensity that moves everyone who hears. They are listening to a young pianist who could one day be one of Australia's greatest musicians—fourteen-year-old David Helfgott . . . He is believed to be the youngest pianist ever to reach the finals of the ABC competition . . . David squirms with embarrassment when the conversation turns to him . . . He would have been horrified to know that after he appeared on TV many Perth housewives phoned the station to describe David's hands as the most beautiful they had ever seen."

The article by James Penberthy in the Perth *Sunday Times,* which started the whole ball rolling, also included a feature about the family. "The Helfgott family is rich in pride, talent, and happiness," Penberthy wrote, "but they have barely enough money for the necessities of life. Proud papa, Peter Helfgott, a State Electricity Commission fitter, has a wife and five young children to support. Margaret, sixteen, who plays the piano with great dash, passed the Junior Certificate with nine subjects. Leslie, ten, plays Paganini on the violin without any teaching. Eight-year-old Susanna, also untaught, played some Rimsky-Korsakov on the piano. Baby Louisa, just nineteen months, only listens with interest to the others.

"How Polish-born Peter and Rae Helfgott keep their family happy, well-fed, dressed, and educated in their humble home, is quite beyond me," Penberthy added. "Peter Helfgott told me: 'We wanted to maintain some [musical] life in the house so we managed to keep up payments on the piano.' The Helfgotts are with justification a proud family—they ask help from no one."

After a while, my father went to the Perth *Sunday*

Times office to find out how much money had been raised to send David to the United States. But hardly anything had come in. Although a donation had been sent from as far away as Canberra, and a prominent Perth businessman, Alec Breckler, had generously offered to help, the sum raised was far short of that needed. David's move to America was therefore not a realistic option.

To suggest, as *Shine* does, that my father had "refused" David permission to go to the States, and to hint that it was what his family had been through during the Holocaust that had led him to make this irrational and unfair decision—one that would ultimately lead to David's breakdown and institutionalization—is not only a terrible slur on my father but also indirectly on all Holocaust survivors and their descendants.

The whole thing was all in fact a case of misinterpretation. The media, taking their cue from the *Sunday Times,* wrongly reported or implied that Stern and Simon had actually made a concrete offer to David to study in the United States. In reality, they had merely praised his playing and suggested, in an off-the-cuff kind of way, that he should consider going abroad to study.

Isaac Stern was furious at the way *Shine* misrepresented what happened—in scene 21 of the published screenplay, the film refers to an "invitation" by Stern—and he was surprised that Scott Hicks had not even consulted him about this. Stern even told journalists in 1997, after *Shine* came out, that he had never made any firm offer to David Helfgott.

However, in 1961, the young David, at once arrogant and naive, and caught up in the frenzy of all the press attention, let his imagination run wild. He even convinced himself that he was actually going to live in Stern's home in America.

James Penberthy and others in Perth musical circles, eager to put the city on the map as far as classical music was concerned, were very keen that David follow Simon and Stern's advice. But while my father shared their hopes and enthusiasm, he also had to take account of parental concerns. He knew that David was incapable of looking after himself. He told those who were making an effort to raise funds that if they enabled the whole family to go to America, then he would have no objection, because we would be there to look after David. But as a father he couldn't allow a young son—especially one with problems—to go off on his own and fend for himself on the other side of the world.

My mother, my brother, and my sisters all think my father was right, as do I. To suggest, as *Shine* does, that my father was in some way mean-spirited is totally unfair. Holding back David's career was not in the least my father's aim. He was extremely proud of his son and nurtured his talent in every way. He was David's strongest advocate. But allowing any boy who had just turned fourteen to live by himself so far away without proper provisions being made for him would have been irresponsible, to say the least.

In David's case, it would have been particularly inappropriate. He had never been abroad before; he was completely hopeless in practical matters; and he needed to be looked after, cooked for, and cared for.

He was also by that time behaving rather erratically, although of course we did not know then that these may have been the first signs of a serious mental illness. My father's attitude was proved correct: when David did go to London of his own volition four years later, he fell ill and ended up receiving psychiatric care.

In any case there simply wasn't enough money available to finance the trip to America. Contrary to what is related in *Shine,* where my father and Mr. Rosen decide that David should have a bar mitzvah as a method of raising money for this trip, David had already had his bar mitzvah almost a year earlier, when he turned thirteen, the usual age for this ceremony. His bar mitzvah had nothing to do with "digging for gold," as Mr. Rosen puts it in *Shine,* in one of several offensive references in the film to Jews or Judaism. My father may not have been an Orthodox Jew himself, but he still had a strong desire to hold onto the basic tenets of Jewish tradition and to pass them on to his children.

So, with insufficient money forthcoming with which to fund the trip, the whole American proposal inevitably came to nothing. However, the atmosphere created by the press, even though it had no real basis in fact, had raised David's hopes sky high. I remember my father tactfully trying to explain all this to David. But my brother had been so excited at the prospect of going that he didn't really take it all in, and, in part at least, blamed his father for the "offer" not materializing—as though it were my father's fault that he didn't have enough money to pay for David to go and live in America.

*   *   *

After the Isaac Stern episode and its aftermath, the relationship between David and my father became less close. We were still not sure, however, whether David's gradual withdrawal from the family wasn't simply the kind of difficult phase that many adolescents go through. I was becoming more independent myself at this time, and went to work in Melbourne— though there was of course a huge difference between my spending a few weeks in Melbourne, under the watchful eye of my grandparents, and the idea of David, who was two years younger than me and considerably less mature—he still could not even tie his own shoelaces—spending years alone on the other side of the world.

Although his attitude was troublesome, once he had got over the disappointment of the America trip that never was, David's musical skills continued to improve. I was amazed at the sensitive way in which he could now interpret some of the works he mastered. For example, he played Prelude No. 8 by Bach (from the first book of Preludes and Fugues) very tenderly; this slow, quiet, and introspective piece required him to demonstrate a range of skills quite different from those required to play the more lively and virtuoso pieces by Liszt, Rachmaninoff, and Balakirev, which David usually performed.

In October 1961, David achieved a remarkable result for a fourteen-year-old. He scored 184 out of 200 as he successfully passed the exam for his certificate of Associate in Music, and he was awarded the special annual prize by the Australian Music Examinations Board.

We continued going to concerto competitions and the papers eagerly followed David's musical successes. Many articles about David were accompanied by a photograph of him wearing a jacket and bow tie, looking serious and confident behind his thick-rimmed spectacles and half smile.

By now his reputation had been established well beyond Perth. Under the headline "Professor: Helfgott is 'Great Pianist,'" an article in a Melbourne newspaper began: "Professor Sidney Harrison said yesterday that young Perth pianist David Helfgott was among the best and most talented artists he had seen in twenty-five years as an adjudicator. The world-famous music authority said 'David, at fourteen, was far, far the youngest competitor in the [ABC Concerto] competition. All the judges agreed he has an extraordinary talent . . . Harrison, professor of music at the Guildhall School of Music in London said David's rendition of Mozart's concerto was faultless. 'When I return to England in July I shall certainly mention David Helfgott as a great young Australian pianist,' he added."

"An enormous talent," declared the Dutch conductor Willem van Otterloo in an article about David that appeared in 1962. Another critic wrote about "the magic in the brilliant fingers of David Helfgott."

I still have newspaper clippings about David's performances of Rachmaninoff's Third Piano Concerto in Perth on June 16, 1964 and in Melbourne on July 4, 1964. The critic Sally Trethowan wrote of the Perth performance: "Under his talented hands this work exploded in a display of aural pyrotechnics that brought long and enthusiastic applause from the large audience."

Another critic, Adrian Rawlins, said: "Helfgott played the Rachmaninoff Concerto with great sensitivity and insight."

(Scott Hicks, in what he has referred to in interviews as the "ten-year odyssey" it took to research and make *Shine,* could surely have found out—if not from David or a library, then by speaking to my mother, Leslie, or me—that David had mastered Rachmaninoff's Third Piano Concerto at least five years before the 1969 London performance that, Hicks alleges, caused David to collapse on stage and led to a major breakdown.)

Year after year—and in marked contrast to the reviews David has recently been receiving—music critics were almost unanimous in their praise of David's performances. In May 1965, for example, *The Sunday Times* (Perth) ran an article under the headline "Born to a Piano." "Helfgott dazzles" was the heading of a piece by Barbara Yates Rothwell in another paper.

But, as David received more and more praise, his head swelled even larger. His arrogance continued to increase until he left for London in 1966. The whole family felt the changes. As my little sister Suzie said, David's attitude at the time was "I'm better than anyone." At one point, totally out of the blue, he actually stopped talking to me altogether. Then one day, he wanted me to type up a poem for him, which I did willingly—I thought he had got over whatever it was he was holding against me. However, after I gave David back the typed-up poem, to my absolute astonishment, he promptly stopped talking to me again. I was flabbergasted.

7

STALIN, MAO, AND TABLE TENNIS

There was more to life in the Helfgott household than music. David and my father shared a keen interest in politics. They were both on the left of the political spectrum and believed that socialism was the way to achieve equality and justice. Sometimes they had heated discussions about which brand of socialism was best, Russian or Chinese.

My father had finally become disillusioned with Russian socialism as a result of the "Doctors' Plot" of 1953, when Stalin accused his Jewish doctors of trying to poison him. This was a total fabrication, intended to prepare the way for a vicious wave of anti-Semitic persecution across the whole Soviet Union. Stalin announced that his doctors were part of "an international Jewish bourgeois-nationalist organization established by American intelligence." He then had his doctors tortured in order to extract confessions from them.

The official Communist Party newspaper *Pravda* described the Jewish doctors as "the pack of mad dogs from Tel Aviv," which it characterized as "loathsome and vile in its thirst for blood." After this my father finally made the break with Russia and decided that Chairman Mao's Chinese socialism was far more pure and correct; David meanwhile still adhered to a belief in the Russian variety as "the true socialism."

Even though my father no longer sympathized with Soviet communism, he nevertheless kept an eye on developments in the communist world. He and David would visit the left-wing Pioneer Bookshop in Perth, and buy magazines called *Soviet Union* and *Red China* (the latter may have been called *Pictorial China*—I can't now recall for certain). *Red China* was overflowing with propaganda. Each issue seemed to be filled with pictures of smiling, rosy-cheeked girls picking apples in the field, or carrying baskets bursting with agricultural produce.

Australia had its own Communist Party, and David struck up a friendship with Katherine Susannah Pritchard, one of its founding members. But while he sometimes went to her house for dinner, neither he nor my father ever joined the Communist Party, nor, as far as I am aware, did they ever go to the Soviet Friendship Society, as they are shown doing in *Shine*.

David always yearned to visit the Soviet Union and see the situation there for himself. In 1986, by which time Mikhail Gorbachev was in power, he got his wish. He visited music conservatories and took in the sights in Moscow and Leningrad. He returned to Russia in 1993, after communism had collapsed, and gave a small recital of Mussorgsky's "Pictures at an

Exhibition" at Rimsky-Korsakov's home in St. Petersburg, which is now a museum. That year he also visited what had been one of the world's last bastions of hardline communism, Albania, and performed Rachmaninoff's Second Piano Concerto at the Tirana Opera House accompanied by the Albanian Symphony Orchestra.

Politics is still one of my brother's chief interests. In particular, he closely follows events in Russia and Israel, reading news magazines such as *Time* and watching CNN International. When he visited me in Israel in 1988, I was very impressed by his in-depth knowledge of the intricacies of Israeli political life.

Although he loved talking to my father, outside the house David was not very sociable. As a teenager, he was somewhat of a loner. He neither had nor sought many playmates. Life essentially revolved around one thing: the piano. It was practice, practice, practice. He wanted to begin playing as early as four a.m., although Dad would not let him.

By now my father and mother, rather than pushing or coaxing my brother toward more playing, were becoming concerned that David did not have enough other interests or social contact outside the family. He had the odd friend here and there, but not many. Dad tried to encourage him to develop a closer friendship with a boy who lived down the road, called Boris. David played tennis with Boris on a couple of occasions, but after a while, rather than turning up for meetings with his friend, David was back at his beloved piano, mastering Balakirev's "Islamey" or some other fiendishly difficult work.

When, at the age of fifteen, I temporarily lost my enthusiasm for playing the piano, I took up classical and modern ballet, and later acting, squash, jazz piano, and yoga. David, on the other hand, spent what spare time he had on his own. He loved reading science books. One of his favorites was Fred Hoyle's *Astronomy,* which had extraordinary pictures of galaxies. When David was interviewed on the radio and asked what he wanted to be when he grew up, he said a concert pianist or a conductor. But failing that, he said, his third choice was to be an astronomer.

Insofar as there was life for David away from the piano, it was mainly with myself, my brother, and my sisters. We all loved playing table tennis and were very good at it. Our brown table tennis table traveled with us on the boat from Melbourne, and together with the Rönish piano, it remained our most treasured family possession. Now battered and old, it is, like the piano, still being used by Leslie and his family in Perth.

David's hands, so brilliant on the piano keys, were almost as skillful at table tennis. He favored the grip used by the Chinese, wrapping his thumb and index finger around the handle. Rallies with him were always a challenge. He could put a vicious spin on the ball and, given half a chance, would smash it extremely hard at his opponent, leaving me panting for breath as I raced from side to side trying to return his shots.

Meanwhile, David's behavior continued to grow stranger. For example, he became absolutely obsessive about germs. He would refuse to touch taps or

sink areas, even at home. When he went to the bathroom he would pry the tap open with a fork, and
then, after he had washed his hands, he would take
even greater care to close it without touching it, petrified that he might pick up fresh germs.

In spite of the tension caused by David's sometimes unpleasant behavior toward us, we still managed to go on enjoyable family outings during this
period. We often took the train to the port of
Fremantle, twelve miles south of Perth, which is
where the Swan River flows into the Indian Ocean.
We did not only go to "Freo"—as it is affectionately
known by locals—just to have a pleasant picnic. On
scorching summer days temperatures could rise to
100 degrees Fahrenheit in Perth, and the special
breeze down in the port, known as the "Fremantle
Doctor," provided some welcome relief. All of us,
David included, used to love these trips. We either
brought our own lunch—hard-boiled eggs, salad,
fruit, bread and butter, a thermos of coffee, and fruit
juice—or Mom and Dad would treat us to fish and
chips at the Fisherman's Wharf, which was owned by
Italian immigrants who went out twice daily to bring
back fresh catches.

While eating, the seagulls would surround us and
screech away in their inimitable manner, loudly demanding a share of the meal. We soon learned not to
be too generous in giving away the scraps—unless
we wanted to be bombarded by another hundred
hungry seagulls within a matter of seconds.

After lunch my parents would lie together on the
blanket we brought with us and sometimes they
would cuddle when we children went off to play.

Nearby were the docks where the big ships came in from abroad. We would scurry down there whenever we saw a boat come in. These foreign ships and their crews seemed terribly exotic to us, and we played all kinds of games, dreaming up tales of pirates and fortune hunters. David and I, being the eldest children, would sometimes think about Europe and the ships that our parents had arrived on. We were already old enough to know the fate of those who hadn't made it to Australia—"the lucky country" as it is fondly known by its grateful peoples. These otherwise happy childhood moments were tinged with sadness when we thought of our parents' families and the others who didn't make it.

Another place we used to frequent on family outings was Hyde Park, near our home in Highgate. This was a beautiful place, with manicured lawns and gardens and plenty of benches on which to sit and gaze at the peaceful surroundings. Often on weekends we went there to feed the ducks and swans and stroll around the tranquil lake. Sometimes we also went to King's Park, an area of untouched bush land that Perth's nineteenth-century founders had deliberately preserved in the center of the city. King's Park overlooks the Swan River and is very close to the University of Western Australia. We used to run around amid the gum trees and wildflowers there and take in the magnificent panoramic views.

School naturally played a big part in our lives. In Perth we first went to Highgate State school. Later, when we moved to a working-class area some distance away called Maniana, David and I went to Queen's Park, which was a fairly poor school with many aboriginal children. When we moved back to Highgate, we split up—I studied at Mt. Lawley High School and David went to Forrest High School for Boys.

Romance did not play a large part in David's teenage life. Immersed in music, he didn't seem to be very interested in girls. During the entire period before he left for London at the age of nineteen, I don't recall him going out on a single date—although there was no shortage of female music students who developed crushes on him after hearing the magic he produced at the piano.

I, on the other hand, had reached an age where I wanted to go out with boys. Clothes were always a problem, though. I was quite adept at thinking up all kinds of ways of renovating old clothes so that they would look a little different. I would sew braids on them or embroider them with beads and sequins to give them a fresh burst of life. For instance, I removed some brightly colored buttons from an old cardigan and sewed them on a skirt to create the sort of effect I imagined Gypsies might make.

In the early days in Perth we went to the synagogue fairly regularly, and some members of the Jewish community used to offer us second-hand clothes. Although my father abhorred charity, he did not like to be rude, so he accepted their gifts. I was once given a lovely dress from one of these handouts, and wore it to synagogue for Rosh Hashanah, the Jewish New Year. When a girl came up to me and said, "Oh, I used to have a dress just like that," I felt mortified. I could have sunk through the floor. I quickly made up a not particularly credible story about my parents having just bought me the dress from some shop. I wanted to save myself from the shame of receiving handouts. It was only many years later that I realized that charity could be a good thing. Indeed, Judaism dictates that one should give 10 percent of one's income to the less fortunate. At the time, however, I merely felt like a victim of poverty, and this was a terrible source of embarrassment.

Despite my discomfort about my clothes, I went out on my first date when I was sixteen. I was asked out by a very handsome boy, who was three years older than me. He took me to a drive-in movie— these were very popular in Perth because of the city's warm weather. There were two full-length feature films on the program and by the time they ended it was fairly late. But since we were famished, we joined two other couples for a quick late-night bite at Bernie's Hamburger joint on Riverside Drive, next to the Swan River.

When he dropped me home, the boy, who I thought was absolutely gorgeous, asked me if I would like to go to a party with him the next evening. Thrilled that he seemed to like me, I could hardly get the word "yes" out quickly enough. But when I went through our front door, much later than planned, I found Dad waiting up for me, worried about his precious eldest daughter.

"You can't go," Dad said to me when I told him I had already accepted a date for a party the next night. My father was very angry about my coming home so late without warning him. But on the following evening, being a defiant teenager, I waited till my father and David left the house to go to a concert in which David was playing, got dressed, and concocted a dummy body for my bed, made up of blankets and pillows to give the appearance of a sleeping person. I then swore the whole household to secrecy. "Don't you dare tell anyone," I cautioned my little brother and sister sternly.

When my father came home with David, he peeked into the bedroom I shared with Suzie, saw the dummy, and presumed I was asleep. Some months later I discovered that my mother had told him the truth and that in any case he had not been fooled by the dummy, but had decided to play along with my prank. Perhaps he was rewarding me for my boldness and initiative, or perhaps he thought there was no point in trying to control his rebellious teenage daughter and that to discipline me would only make things worse.

All in all, I was going through quite a rebellious phase. For example, my father didn't like me wearing makeup. "Natural beauty is far better than artificial beauty," he told me. But I went ahead and smeared myself with all sorts of colors, just to show Dad that I would do what I liked. Not surprisingly, he went off in a huff when I did.

My mother at this time had her hands full with my four younger siblings, including a two-year-old baby. So, in search of a sympathetic female ear to listen to my woes about boys and other adolescent problems, I turned to my younger sister Suzie. Although she was eight years my junior, Suzie possessed an understanding and maturity well beyond her years. She would listen patiently to my concerns and then give me her advice: "Mom and Dad will be furious if they see you in that new green eye makeup"; "You should choose this boy because he treats you nicely, rather than that one who is better looking," she would say. Although Suzie spent most of her time at this age playing with friends, she was already a good listener and giver of advice, skills that served her well later in her career as a social worker.

Meanwhile, my youngest sister Louise, although only two years old at the time, was beginning to make her presence felt. Her curiosity knew no bounds. She would muster up all the energy in her tiny body and haul the large science and nature books off our shelves. She would turn over the pages, studying the pictures diligently. The next step was reading and writing, which she learned very quickly. She began writing poems at the age of seven and never looked back. Many of her poems have been published, and the plays she has written have been performed. Her latest work, a musical called *The Bridge,* about destitute street kids, was staged in July 1997 in the theater in Mandurah, a town one hour's drive south of Perth. Among my favorite of Louise's poems is *Freudian Slips,* a humorous account of Freud's "trek through the jungle of the psyche," and another one that explores the way people communicate, or don't communicate, when they sit opposite each other in trains.

I left school at the age of fifteen and spent three years working as a secretary in a big shoe shop. It never occurred to me to go on to higher education because I knew this wasn't financially feasible. As the eldest child, I also knew my contribution would greatly help my parents. So my wages were divided into board for my parents and of course a portion for myself. As soon as I received my paycheck every week, I would rush out and buy myself a new piece of clothing—a cardigan, a skirt, stockings, or a pair of shoes. It was a great feeling finally to start buying my own things and to become independent.

I had some brief periods away from home. At sixteen, I stayed in Melbourne with my grandparents for a few weeks and took part in the Jewish Sports Carnival. I was picked to play on the girls' hockey team representing the Jewish Community of Western Australia, though I was in fact a very poor hockey player, running away if the ball came at me too hard. But I had great fun at the two-week carnival and made many new friends.

Two years later I returned to Melbourne for several weeks and worked for a fashion business. Upon my return to Perth, I worked for two years for a firm that supplied paint, easels, and drawing equipment for artists. I used to love the aroma of the paint, and the artistic types who would wander in and browse among the glowing colors. After that, from 1965 to 1968, I worked as a check-typist for the State Electricity Commission (SEC) of Western Australia. My father had already been working at the SEC for many years as an electrical fitter in the meter shop, and Leslie also started working for them as an electrician in 1966. Although we all worked for the same government department, we didn't see each other much at work, because our workplaces were in different locations.

My father worked in the meter shop until he retired in 1968 at the age of sixty-five. He is famous among his workmates for bringing his violin in to play. At first they wouldn't believe a blue-collar worker could play a classical instrument. Dave Bowron, the chief engineer in charge of the meter shop, told my brother Leslie recently: "We didn't really believe Peter could play, so we dared him to bring his violin in. But when he took up the challenge and brought in his fiddle we were all very impressed."

It was only in my early twenties that I decided to go back to studying, taking my Associate in Music exams, which were issued by the Australian Music Examinations Board, under the auspices of the University of Western Australia. Previously I had thought that higher education was only for the very rich or for students gifted enough to obtain a scholarship, and it had never occurred to me when I left school that I could do something more ambitious. Later, at the age of thirty, when I moved to Israel, I took a bachelor of arts degree in History and English Language at the Hebrew University of Jerusalem.

David, too, left high school after earning his Junior Certificate, even though my parents very much wanted him to stay on and obtain his Leaving (Higher School) Certificate. But he was obsessed with the piano; he just wanted to devote his entire life to it.

Louise, my youngest sister, was the only one of us who stayed on at school beyond the age of fifteen and then continued her education at university where she gained bachelor's degrees in psychology and creative writing. Suzie, like me, took a break. She left school young, worked for a few years, and then later went on to higher education. She took a degree in social work at the University of Western Australia and now helps adults with alcohol and drug problems. Leslie, who left school with a very respectable score of eight subjects for his Junior Certificate, is a qualified electrician, but now earns his income as a musician.

Although there were many material things that I craved in my childhood, I realize now that growing up poor is not without its benefits. I will always appreciate being able to enjoy material comforts—buying clothes and so on—in a way that I might not have done had we always taken such things for granted. And growing up without many possessions also meant there was a much greater emphasis on enriching our childhood in other ways—from music to chess to acrobatics—for which I am truly grateful.

8

PETER AND DAVID ARGUE
AND MAKE UP

One day, out of the blue, David announced to my father that he intended to go and live in England. His plan was to study at the Royal College of Music in London to work toward a performer's diploma. David said that he had already been talking for some time to several members of the Jewish community whom my father didn't know. They had agreed the idea was a good one, indeed they may even have thought it up themselves; and they had promised to help organize and fund the trip. David said he had also been discussing the plan with Frank Callaway, professor of music at the University of Western Australia.

My father had mixed feelings about David leaving. He wanted the best for his son's career, which he himself had done so much to foster. But he also knew that David's behavior was not quite normal, and he was worried about what might happen when he was left to look after himself alone in London, a city so much bigger and more cosmopolitan than Perth. But as they talked, he could see how much David had set his sights on going. It was 1966, David was now eighteen and no longer a child, and though he was still legally a minor (under Australian law at the time, the age of majority was twenty-one), my father felt that in practice he had the right to decide for himself.

One thing my father could not abide, though, was the idea of other people interfering in his son's life behind his back. David told my father that some members of the Jewish community, eager to become involved in the life of Perth's "star musician," had decided to organize a "charity concert in aid of David Helfgott." My father was a proud man who did not like the idea of his family receiving charity, especially when he had not asked for it—and in this case he had not even been told about it. He was not at all happy about the idea of his son being, as he saw it, paraded publicly as an object of charity.

It seemed to him that the tight-knit Perth Jewish community included one or two individuals who, though no doubt well-meaning, were overstepping the mark in involving themselves in other people's affairs. In the old *shtetls* of eastern Europe, no family event was private. The individual was submerged in the wider community, and family sorrows as well as family joys were shared by the community as a whole, which felt it had a right and a duty to make its opinions known. Some of these attitudes were carried over to Australian Jewry, and various individuals felt they still had the right to busy themselves in the family affairs of other members of the community—in this case Peter's—as they saw fit.

Peter was not against David going to London per se, and certainly not against his receiving the best possible training to further his musical potential. What concerned him was that people, whom he didn't know and who he believed didn't really understand David and his special needs, were making arrangements on David's behalf without consulting him.

I remember vividly David and my father sitting around the kitchen table one night discussing David's trip. My father said: "Look, if you really want to go to London we'll fix it up, we'll arrange it for you. But we'll do it in a proper way. You don't have to go to others and ask for charity." Just as my father had quickly recognized David's deep desire to go to London, so David understood my father's distress that it was being arranged without his involvement. The two of them—who, despite their differences, were still probably the closest members of the family—reached an understanding: David would drop the "charity concert," while my father, who had his own contacts in the music world, promised that he would arrange a farewell concert for David at the Capitol Theater. It would be a regular concert for the paying public, not a charity event.

It therefore came as a great surprise to my father when a little while later, after he had begun making inquiries about organizing a concert, he opened *The Maccabean,* the Perth Jewish newspaper, and read the following: "A charity concert will be held on the 17th of May in aid of David Helfgott."

Despite their agreement, David had apparently continued to plan a charity concert rather than allow my father to organize a regular one. Much of what happened next is described in a lengthy letter that my father wrote to Professor Callaway on April 13, 1966. In the letter he says that he was upset because no one had asked David's parents whether they thought such a charity concert in aid of their son was a good idea. The wording of the announcement for the concert, he wrote, "sounded to me like David is starving and he needs some aid."

My father told Callaway that he had written to *The Maccabean* and asked the editor who had been responsible for placing the announcement. In his opinion the newspaper should not have had it printed without first consulting him since his son was still legally a minor.

A few days later my father received a letter from a Mrs. Green (not her real name), one of the organizers of the charity concert. In her letter, she lectured my father on "human morality, how a father should do things, and how wrong you have been in writing to the editor of the newspaper and expressing your indignation." My father wrote back to Mrs. Green, telling her (as he explained in his letter to Professor Callaway) that he was not interested in her "good intentions of running a concert for David's benefit."

Another woman actually came to see my father and informed him it was she who had put the announcement in *The Maccabean*. "You can't cancel the concert. I may lose my job," she said. She told my father to leave things as they were and not interfere. She then became very offensive and abusive—"most unladylike," as he put it in his letter to Callaway. He added that "it's not my way of treating a lady, but I had to walk out of the room and leave her."

My father makes clear in his letter to Callaway that he was not against a fund-raising concert or opposed to David going to London. "If they had asked me in a proper manner, I cannot see why I should not have consented to the concert, but I did not like them to arrange things without giving me the slightest hint about it."

I typed this letter for him and still have a copy. Had Scott Hicks agreed to speak to me when concocting his "true story," I would have been more than happy to let him see it.

When my father confronted David and reproached him for having broken their agreement by secretly continuing discussions about the charity concert, they got into a big argument that was witnessed by the whole family, myself included. But the way in which this argument is depicted in *Shine*—it is a crucial turning point in the film, where the character of Peter is extremely violent toward David and swears never to speak to him again—is utterly untrue.

Firstly, the argument was not about whether David should study in London, an idea that my father had already accepted. It was about the way in which David had deceived him and about the way my father had found out about it. Dad picked up a copy of *The Maccabean* and said angrily, "What's this? You told me you weren't going to go ahead with this." He paced back and forth in the living room, emphasizing how upset he was that David had gone behind his back. David shouted back that he wanted the charity concert. The rest of us sat quietly on the sofa, watching in disbelief as my father and my brother shouted at each other for fifteen minutes.

Secondly, although the argument was certainly unpleasant, there was no swearing or physical violence. My father never once hit David or threatened to hit him. I am not the only one who is absolutely certain of this. My mother and siblings are equally sure. As Suzie says, "Dad was never physically violent."

Thirdly, David was not thrown out of the house by his father on the night of the supposed beating, nor did he leave as a result of it. David had already packed his suitcase before the argument, having decided to take up an invitation to stay with one of the organizers of his trip to London, Mrs. Edna Luber-Smith, president of the Perth branch of the Australian Council of Jewish Women. After the argument, David just picked up his suitcase and went down the street to nearby Mt. Lawley, where the Luber-Smiths lived.

Finally, the idea that my father never spoke to, or threatened never to speak to, David again is ridiculous. The character who represents my father in *Shine* says: "You cruel, callous, stupid boy . . . If you go, you will never come back into this house again. You will never be anybody's son . . . You want to destroy this family! . . . You will not step outside that door. You will be punished for the rest of your life!!" My father said nothing of the sort. He and David remained in close regular contact both during and after David's time in London. When David returned to Perth, he came back to live with us.

Callaway is a man much respected in international music circles. In 1997, he won the highly prestigious

UNESCO Music Prize, previous winners of which include Dimitri Shostakovich, Yehudi Menuhin and
Leonard Bernstein, and he was hailed by UNESCO as
"one of the great pioneers and ambassadors of music
education of our time." After *Shine* was released,
Callaway told my brother Leslie and myself that he remembers the meeting that took place around that
time with my father and David in his office at the university. He said that my father was perfectly pleasant
and calm throughout. As a minor, David had to have
his parents' permission to study abroad. Callaway
said: "Your father was perfectly willing to sign the papers. He did so without any tension or problem at all.
Peter just gave his blessing and wished David all the
best and he signed the necessary papers for David to
go and study in London."

Professor Callaway, who was knighted by Queen
Elizabeth II in 1981 for his services to Australian and
international music, said: "As for David, I had no idea
at the time he was mentally unbalanced. I just
thought he was highly excitable." Callaway told me
that neither Hicks nor anyone else involved in the
making of *Shine* ever contacted him, though he
would have been more than willing to speak about
David and his decision to study in London.

The entire family believed that my father was in the
right. Of course David was not under an obligation to
inform Dad of his plans, but it would have been the
decent thing to do, especially after all that my father
had done for him.

For David's part, it seems he may still have been
harboring some resentment toward my father for the
failure of his trip to America after Isaac Stern's visit.

So when people outside the family suggested that he be sent overseas, he was particularly receptive to the idea. For him, England, as a European country, and as the home of composers such as Edward Elgar and Benjamin Britten, was one of the great centers of classical music.

Although we could understand David's excitement, we realized that our father was justified in his opposition to the trip. Leslie says: "Dad was 100 percent correct—although of course Professor Callaway and Mrs. Luber-Smith are no more to blame for David's subsequent breakdown than my father. I am sure they had nothing but good intentions. However, it is usually more appropriate for people to consult with the parents than with the children."

Suzie says: "Dad did oppose David going to England, but so did the whole family. Dad knew how young and vulnerable David was; he knew he would not be able to manage on his own. It was interfering outsiders who didn't understand that."

Another person who remembers this period well is Madame Alice Carrard. By the time these events occurred, she had been David's principal piano teacher for about three years—Frank Arndt had stepped aside when David was fifteen, feeling that he had taught David all he could. Madame Carrard spent more time with my brother during this period than anyone else outside the family. As with Professor Callaway, Hicks did not speak to her when making *Shine,* although she tells me she would have been happy to inform him about the truth of what happened.

Widely respected as the "grand old lady" of Perth's musical circles, Madame Carrard arrived in Perth in

1942, bringing with her the rich musical traditions of her native Hungary and the historical grandeur of the Austro-Hungarian Empire. Both David and I were extremely privileged to receive her unique musical training. It was under Carrard's tutelage that, in June 1964, David gave a virtuoso performance of Rachmaninoff's Third Piano Concerto, accompanied by the West Australian Symphony Orchestra.

She celebrated her 100th birthday in Perth in April 1997 by giving a recital of Beethoven's Piano Sonata, opus 111, and then treating the audience to a burst of Bela Bartok, the great Hungarian composer with whom she had studied piano in Budapest at the age of sixteen. Carrard, who had a flourishing career as a concert pianist, used to tell me about "the shivers that ran down my back when Bartok gazed at me with his penetrating beautiful brown eyes."

Madame Carrard became David's piano teacher again in the 1970s and still remains in close touch with him. She knows him very well and cares deeply about him. She is a remarkable woman who still plays the piano daily and is now believed to be the world's oldest piano teacher. Despite her age, she retains sharp recollections of all the difficulties surrounding David's trip.

On a visit to Perth in the second half of 1996, I went to pay my respects to Madame Carrard, who at the time was ill in hospital. She had seen and disliked *Shine,* but even I was unprepared for the vehemence with which she defended my father. "Sending David to London was tantamount to sending him to commit suicide," she said, attacking those members of the

Perth Jewish community who had failed to show consideration for my father's views.

Later, in May 1997, when I was back in Israel and had decided to write this book, I asked my brother Leslie and his wife Marie to interview Madame Carrard to get a fuller grasp of her view of what had occurred during this period. They sent me the cassettes of that interview. "I was against David going abroad," she says. "Why? Because David was never normal! I think he was born with that mental problem. His father and I instinctively knew this.

"I've seen the film. It's fiction, fiction, fiction. It's all fiction. There was not much Peter Helfgott could do. Everything was organized behind his back and David wanted to go to London. Peter knew David better than anyone. He realized David should not be left alone. David was a very sick person and not very reliable. His father was right, but David wasn't listening. He thought that there would always be someone looking after him, as there had been in Perth. He didn't realize it wouldn't be good for him to try and cope alone. David was too young and taken in by everybody.

"I was his music teacher and yet the people who organized the trip didn't even come to talk to me!" she added, still surprised by this. "I would have advised against. I knew David's fragile mental state. I knew that he would be lost once he went to London. But I wasn't able to explain this to David because I knew he wouldn't understand why I did not want him to go. I was very sorry that he left.

"There was goodwill there on the part of the Jewish community but they didn't realize that David was a very sick person. I don't know what Mrs. Luber-Smith was thinking of."

Madame Carrard continues: "His stay in England was a complete failure. He was no good, he missed his lessons. He missed history lessons and theory lessons and he was just lost. I can't understand why his father let him go at all."

Nevertheless, my father reconciled himself to the fact that David was going. After the argument, David stayed with Phillip and Edna Luber-Smith for a short while before he left for England. My parents were not angry with him for doing this. They realized that on reaching adulthood children sometimes need to put distance between themselves and their family, as indeed I had already done when I went to Melbourne. David made regular visits back home while he was staying at the Luber-Smiths' and my parents would give him some fruit, some money, or whatever he needed.

In recalling David's stay with her, Mrs. Luber-Smith remembered David's untidiness; how he would eat with his fingers rather than a knife and fork; and how he preferred to eat at the piano, which he was loath to leave, rather than at the table.

Since the original organizers refused to cancel their concert, my father had to drop his plans to hold one at the Capitol Theater. The concert organized by the National Council of Jewish Women of Australia went ahead on May 17, 1966, two days before David's nineteenth birthday, although the word "charity" was dropped from the program.

In addition to the money raised from the concert, David received a grant from the university music department toward his fare, tuition, fees, and living expenses. Another Jewish charitable organization, the Phineas Seeligson Trust, provided David with the clothes he needed for London, including a tailored suit, an overcoat, and various pairs of smart shoes. (David only won a scholarship from the Royal College of Music three years into his course, which gave him the right to study for a fourth year.)

The program for David's farewell concert read as follows:

RECITAL
by
DAVID HELFGOTT
PIANIST
GOVERNMENT HOUSE BALLROOM
PERTH
Tuesday, 17th May, 1966
at 8 p.m.
in the presence of His Excellency the Governor,
Sir Douglas Kendrew
and Lady Kendrew
Arranged by
The National Council of Jewish Women of Australia,
Perth section

The program notes read as follows:

"DAVID HELFGOTT
Tonight's concert is the latest milestone in the career of nineteen-year-old David Helfgott who will soon be leaving to study at the Royal College of Music, London. He has recently been awarded

an overseas bursary by the Music Council of
W.A., a scholarship by the Music Examinations
Board of the University of Western Australia and
a grant from the Phineas Seeligson Trust of Perth.

David is well-known to Perth audiences for his
many performances at concerts and music festivals, and on radio and TV. He received his first
piano lessons at the age of five from his father.
At nine he played a Chopin Polonaise at a country music festival and at twelve he entered the
ABC Concerto competition for the first time,
playing the Bach D Minor Concerto. The following year he was selected as a State Finalist and
gained second place with the Ravel G Minor
Concerto. The succeeding three years saw him
State winner, first with the Mozart C Minor
Concerto, then with the Liszt E-flat Major, and finally at the age of seventeen with the
Rachmaninoff D Minor Concerto.

David holds both Associate and Licentiate cer-
tificates of the AMEB and won the Vincent
Memorial prize for the best results in Associate
with 184 marks out of a possible 200. Visiting
celebrities for whom he has played and who
have predicted a brilliant future for him include
Julius Katchen, Louis Kentner, Isaac Stern, Gina
Bachauer, Abbey Simon, Tamas Vasary, and
Daniel Barenboim. David is at present studying
with Mme. Alice Carrard."

That evening, following the National Anthem,
David performed works by Beethoven, Schumann,
Chopin, Liszt, and Mussorgsky. The packed hall gave

him a standing ovation. It was a true moment of glory and an appropriate musical send-off.

Three months later, on August 14, David set sail from Fremantle for London on the *Himalaya,* which would be making a brief stop in Egypt before arriving in London a month later. David's dreams of leaving Australia were finally being realized. As he set sail with both excitement and trepidation, none of us could know what triumphs and disasters awaited him.

9

DAVID IN LONDON—A STORY THAT CANNOT BE FULLY TOLD

David lived in London for four years, from September 1966 to August 1970. Throughout this time relations between father and son remained close. The suggestion made in *Shine* that there was a total breakdown in communication is preposterous; they wrote to each other regularly. David also wrote to my mother and to all his siblings—and we all wrote back. David's letters were never sent back unopened by my father marked "Return to Sender," as is shown in the film. Nor did my father burn his collection of press clippings about David. David himself now has the originals—I borrowed them and made photocopies in the 1980s.

The correspondence between David and my father reveals enormous love and affection. The letters begin along the lines of "Dear Dad, it was super to get your letter; it made me very happy" (letter of

November 11, 1969), and end with such expressions of unqualified love as "Cheerio for now, Dad, all my love and affection, your loving son, David," or "From the bottom of my heart, all my love and affection, David."

When my father died in 1975, he was living with David, Leslie, Louise, and my mother in the house that Leslie had bought in South Perth in 1971. He left to Leslie the letters that David wrote from London. The publication in full of these letters, in David's own handwriting, would establish once and for all that *Shine* is based on lies. Yet they cannot be published for one reason: the obstructive attitude of David's second wife, Gillian.

Gillian Murray, a divorcee, first met David in 1983, eight years after my father passed away. She married David a year later. She is one of the principal sources for *Shine,* collaborating closely with Scott Hicks throughout his "ten-year odyssey." She provided him with a great deal of information, and even went so far as to be present on the set during the filming of some scenes.

Her spin-off book of the film, *Love You to Bits and Pieces,* described on its front cover as "The true story that inspired the movie *Shine,*" has become an international best-seller. In it, she not only repeats many of the falsehoods told in *Shine,* but adds some new ones of her own. She seems happy to vilify my father even though she never met him. Either she defames him directly or she does so by quoting what she claims David has said. However, I believe it is highly doubtful that David actually spoke the words attributed to him; and if he did, I do not believe these genuinely represent his own feelings. David, who after years of psychiatric treatment, is still on constant medication, remains childlike, easy to manipulate, and heavily under Gillian's influence. (Gillian herself even admits at one point in her book that David is "extremely malleable material.")

Here are a few examples of the things said about my father in *Love You to Bits and Pieces:*

- "Peter Helfgott was a helpless, hopeless, sickly father who could do nothing for his son but provide him with a rickety piano and a homemade stool."
- "Peter Helfgott once told his son that he would one day end up 'dead in the gutter.'"
- "Father belted me to the living daylights, he did." (According to Gillian this is David's recollection of the boat trip to Perth in 1953, when he was aged six.)
- "Father burned them all [the letters], set them on fire," Gillian quotes David as supposedly saying. (These particular letters weren't actually written by David to Peter, but are rather letters David had saved from a close friend. Nevertheless this passage certainly suggests my father is the kind of person who would burn someone else's letters.)

In reading these completely fictional statements one soon begins to understand where Hicks found his inspiration for *Shine.* There was, of course, no burning of letters or any other material in the Helfgott household by my father or anyone else. This is the kind of thing the Nazis did.

Yet Gillian's book, in a manner reminiscent of the movie that preceded it, purports to be an "honest" account of David Helfgott's life. *Love You to Bits and Pieces* is, as I write this, still on the best-seller list in a number of countries—which is no doubt the reason why Gillian is now doing her utmost to prevent the publication of David's letters.

Perhaps unaware that copies of the letters still existed at the time she was supplying Hicks with information for *Shine,* Gillian has now panicked. Since learning from an Australian radio program that my brother Leslie had them, she has utilized every means at her disposal to ensure that the true facts be suppressed. First, she persuaded my still mentally fragile brother to sign over to her the copyright of the letters he wrote to his father. Then, in February 1997, she instructed her lawyers to write an extremely hostile letter to Leslie threatening legal action and seeking damages for breach of copyright should we reprint them, warning ominously of "severe sanctions for noncompliance."

International copyright law dictates that while letters themselves are the property of the recipient, who can pass them on to whomever he likes (in this case Leslie), the copyright of the content of a letter remains with the writer. This somewhat strange dichotomy in the area of legal rights means that it is not technically permissible for the owner of a letter to republish it without permission from the copyright holder, in this case Gillian. Since Gillian has prevented their publication, legally we are able only to paraphrase these letters or quote short extracts from them.

I need hardly say that the entire Helfgott family is shocked by Gillian's threats—and bewildered by her unilateral decision to communicate with her family through her lawyers.

If, as Gillian claims, she wants to give an "honest" account of David's life, it is quite beyond me why she has forbidden Leslie and me to reprint letters that show only warmth between David and his father, letters that state: "Dad, I miss you and Mum terribly, I wish you could come over"; and "I only wish you and the family could come over to London. I do miss you and Mum very much"; and "From the bottom of my heart I send you all my love and affection for your 25th wedding anniversary and I'm always thinking of you!" And so on.

It is in these letters that the truth can be found, not in *Love You to Bits and Pieces*.

LONDON LIFE—TRIUMPH AND TRAGEDY

Upon arrival at the Royal College of Music, David—even given the high standard of his fellow students—was judged to be one of the top pupils. He was allocated a grade 4B out of a maximum grade of 5.

The Royal College is one of the world's great conservatories and a wonderful place to study. It was founded in 1883 by royal charter under the presidency of the then Prince of Wales (later King Edward VII). In 1894 it moved from its premises in Kensington Gore to a magnificent Victorian red-brick building on Prince Consort Road, on the southern edge of Hyde Park in London's fashionable Kensington district, and just a few steps away from the Royal Albert Hall.

Among its former pupils, who developed their skills in its resonant and intimate practice rooms, are Benjamin Britten, Barry Douglas, John Lill, Leopold Stokowski, Joan Sutherland, and Michael Tippett.

Students need only browse among the college's valuable collection of antique musical instruments and portraits to gain a sense of its historical importance.

Although David's years in London ended in tragedy, England's capital city was also the scene of a number of his outstanding successes. In 1967, he won first prize for piano in grade 4. In 1968, he won the Marmaduke Barton Prize and the Hopkinson Silver Medal, awarded by the Royal Amateur Orchestral Society, for his performance of Beethoven's D Minor "Tempest" Sonata, Balakirev's "Islamey," and Chopin's Etude op. 25, no. 11. The medal was presented to him the following year by Queen Elizabeth, the Queen Mother. News of David's accolade traveled back to Perth and a photograph of David, head bowed as he meets the Queen Mother, appeared in the local Perth newspapers.

David also began to receive excellent reviews in British papers. In the *Buckinghamshire Examiner* in 1969 under the headline "Pianist Played on Until Midnight," David Chesterman wrote: "When 22-year-old David Helfgott, an Australian pianist, finished his programme at Germains on Sunday, many of the audience refused to go home, and demanded more. He was supplied with coffee and something a little stronger, and he continued playing till after midnight, finishing with that musical Everest, the Liszt Sonata. David Helfgott is a man who, once seated at a piano, moves straight into the world of music, oblivious of everything else . . ."

David was awarded a scholarship in 1969 (after his grant from the University of Western Australia music department ran out), and his professor at the Royal College even compared his technique to that of the world-renowned Russian-born pianist Vladimir Horowitz. David told us about these triumphs in his letters and naturally we were all thrilled.

He also wrote with great enthusiasm about the concerts he attended. "I have been to two Barenboim recitals (all Beethoven sonatas)—what a pianist; and what a personality he's got! He plays superbly," he wrote in one letter. "I've got a ticket for Vladimir Ashkenazy in Brahms's Second Concerto, I'm so excited," he said in another. David told us that on the morning after a concert he would get up early and rush off to buy the score he had heard the night before and then sit in a cafe and study it in detail.

He also kept us informed about his own progress as a musician. In one letter he proudly told how he was going to play at the Wigmore Hall—a small but distinguished venue where many of the world's greatest performers have appeared. David had already mastered composers such as Rachmaninoff and Balakirev prior to his studies at the Royal College of Music; he told us that while in London his aim was to master other composers, of whose work he was not yet in full command. In one of his letters to Dad, he talked about grappling with the intricacies of Liszt, whom he referred to as a "demon." (Many years later, in 1993, David would actually have the opportunity of playing on Liszt's own piano in the composer's former house in Weimar, Germany. He described the occasion at the time as the "most spiritual and moving musical experience of my life.")

David's letters to his siblings, like the ones to his parents, are full of affection. The letters to me begin "Dear Marg" or "Dear Maggie" and usually end "love always" circled by a ring of kisses. (I have been unable to secure permission from Gillian to reprint them.) His letters to Leslie are particularly charming. He asks his younger brother how his violin playing is coming along; in one letter he tells him that he has bought a new sponge-covered table-tennis racket and is looking forward to challenging him to a game next time they meet. Leslie, who collected coins, was absolutely thrilled when David sent him an "Elizabeth I" English shilling dating from 1571 for his birthday.

David also sent us a number of photos from London. We even received one from his stopover in Egypt on his journey to England in which he is smiling and wearing a fez, with several camels sitting idly in the background.

One person who got to know David well while they were both students at the Royal College is Niel Immelman, now professor of piano there. Professor Immelman told me that at that time David seemed to be at the peak of his performing ability as a pianist.

"I first came across David in a practicing room at the Royal College of Music," says Professor Immelman. "He was playing the first solo in the Brahms Second Concerto and I was struck by the sheer physicality of his approach. As I got to know him better, through playing second piano for some of his lessons on Rachmaninoff, I came to admire his lightning-quick reflexes and his outstanding ear. David had supreme technical ability and a flair for public performance. Although he was not overendowed with social skills, his warm, outgoing nature made him very popular with his fellow students. One of his party tricks—and if there was a piano at a party David would spend 90 percent of the time playing it—was to play both the solo and orchestral parts of the Tchaikovsky violin concerto without missing out anything. When asked how long it took him to make this transcription, he replied, 'Oh, I didn't make it, I just play what I hear.'" (David's ability to sight read difficult or complex music without having to practice beforehand, is a rare gift indeed.)

When David arrived in England, the "Swinging Sixties" were at their peak, and with its bright lights and Beatlemania, its shops, museums, theaters and galleries, there were few places more exciting than London. "When David and I were students in the sixties, the Royal College of Music was a friendly and easygoing place," Immelman continues. "Not too much academic work was demanded from those of us on the Performers Course, which left us plenty of time for practicing and concert attendance. David was often seen in the audience at performances by the great pianists of the time such as Arrau, Annie Fischer, Gilels, Richter, and Rubinstein. There was time to reflect and we learned much from discussions with our fellow students in the college canteen and the college pub, affectionately known as 'the 99'— there were only 98 teaching rooms before the new extension was opened in the sixties."

But despite (or perhaps because of) the crowds and excitement, London can be a very lonely and overwhelming place for the outsider from the "back of beyond." In Perth, David had been a local celebrity, a big fish in a small pond. In London, he no longer had just his siblings to compete with, but was surrounded by talented child prodigies and slick, so-phisticated urbanites.

As time went by the tone of David's letters began to change. He seemed to be becoming increasingly dis-tressed and confused, and to be moving frequently from place to place. Initially Hillel, a Jewish student or-ganization, had helped David find accommodation in Willesden, where he rented a room in the house of a Jewish widow, Mrs. Strauss, who also used to cook for him. But after a while, almost every letter seemed to have a new return address. Accustomed to Perth's mild climate, David was having great difficulty in adjusting to the London weather and, perhaps because he wasn't dressing sensibly, he was very cold in the winter.

He was unable to manage his budget properly and so frequently found himself without money. He told us he would spend his last five or ten pounds purchasing a front-row ticket for a Rubinstein concert rather than pay for food or rent. He spent the large sum that it cost at the time to buy contact lenses, but then had no money left for a scarf in winter. He said that he was be-ginning to miss his family and that it wasn't easy for him to be alone in the large and unfamiliar world of London, forced to fend for himself. He even spoke about having terrible nightmares. We were all very wor-ried by these letters, which not only revealed David to be suffering financially, physically, and emotionally, but also seemed to indicate a precarious mental state. Leslie, the next eldest child, remembers this period well: "At first, there was normal communication be-tween David and the family. His breakdown occurred gradually. After a while, he couldn't cope, he was going to pieces. Dad wrote to David very often, trying to help and advise him, and David wrote back regularly. He did not seem to be in a good living environment or to be eating well—at one point he subsisted on a diet of chocolates, milk, and wine. Nor did he seem to have enough money. His letters became erratic and his handwriting strange. We could see changes in his mental state through his letters."

David's letters caused my father tremendous anxiety and pain. He desperately wanted to go and visit his son, but he did not have the financial means to make the trip. We were still too poor to afford a telephone, so we could not even speak to him.

My father's concern reached such a point that he began urging David to return home. Dad wrote to me about this when I was in Melbourne, in a letter dated August 4, 1970: "When David told me in one of his letters that he is sick and of all his troubles, my reply was to pack his bags and come home without a care in the world to worry about. As a matter of fact, I pointed out to him to let me do all the worrying." (A short while later David did actually take up Dad's suggestion and returned home.)

My father wrote to David frequently. Naturally he didn't usually keep copies of his own letters, so we no longer have them. Only one has been found and it provides a little of the flavor of my father's attitude to David. One must bear in mind that English was my father's third language, and his written English was not perfect—he had never been taught formally how to write. The letter, from October 1969, reads as follows:

"Dear, Dear, Dave,

It made us very happy to hear from you so soon, and that your problems are easing off. It is a matter of fact, I had a lot of problems myself, or at least I thought I did, till one day I decided to take control of them . . . So what did I do? I considered every problem and analyzed it from every aspect, and what do you think? I found that I had no problems at all, as happiness doesn't really lie in certain material gains, as sometimes they have the opposite effect—when you got it, you find you don't want it . . .

But I can assure you that with your musical ear and the present knowledge you possess you will have no trouble to enjoy life to the utmost, provided you look after yourself while you are in London alone . . . I'd like to know whether you still keep up your physical exercises. Let us know, all love and kisses from everybody,

Your loving Pop, xxxxx "

Throughout his time in London, David also maintained a regular correspondence with Professor Callaway from the University of Western Australia. At first his letters were warm and enthusiastic, and Callaway was always friendly when he wrote back. He told David about important "milestones in my own musical career" by way of encouragement, and told him to "keep working hard."

But after a while the letters to Professor Callaway, like the ones to his family, displayed mounting distress. Callaway, too, traces David's descent into illness to his period in London. He told me: "I first began to become aware of David's inability to look after himself through the lines of his letters. The reports by his professor, Cyril Smith, also suggested something was afoot. They indicated David's studies were haphazard and regressing. I saw this for myself in 1968–69 when I met David three times during my stay in London. Although he appeared happy in some respects, he also appeared overly excitable and was very worried about money problems."

In 1969, Mr. and Mrs. Luber-Smith went to visit David in London. In recalling her trip later, Mrs. Luber-Smith remembered that by his third year David had started seeing a psychiatrist. She also said that David had found himself living quarters that were crawling with rats and mice, and that he had bought a dilapidated old piano. The place in which he was living, she added, was "awful" but he was very happy as long as he had a piano.

Mrs. Luber-Smith had been surprised when she had gone to a concert in which David was scheduled to perform, but he hadn't turned up. The audience had sat, slightly embarrassed, in the dark while the stage remained empty; one of the organizers had cried out "David Helfgott! David Helfgott!" repeating this again a few minutes later, but there was no response. So the harpist who was due to perform next, had taken David's place on stage. Twenty minutes later David appeared and took over from the harpist. After the concert, Mrs. Luber-Smith asked David where he had been and what had caused the delay. David replied, without any hint that his behavior was out of the ordinary: "I went to have a steak. I was hungry."

This kind of erratic behavior was also observed by Morry Herman, a mathematician from Perth. He remembers visiting relatives in London in 1967. "We were round at some friends for a dinner party and David Helfgott, who was then at the peak of his career, was due to give a private recital. But he dropped his contact lens and all present then spent the entire evening on their hands and knees looking for it, and no music was performed."

David's reports from the Royal College also show a mixed record. They read as follows:

REPORT ON STUDIES, ACADEMIC YEAR 1966–67

Mr. David Helfgott

Subject Piano. Professor Cyril Smith: "He has bursts of brilliant playing, but needs a steadier application to sound work and more attention to basic rhythmic problems."

Composition/Analysis. Mr. Bryan Kelly: "A rather muddled year, a keen pupil but emotion dominates over mind and the results are hectic."

REPORT ON STUDIES, ACADEMIC YEAR 1967–68

Mr. David Helfgott

Subject Piano. Professor Cyril Smith: "He has extraordinary pianistic talent, but his work is ill-organized and spasmodic."

Composition/Analysis. Mr. Bryan Kelly: "Enthusiastic, but convinced that emotion is more important than mind."

REPORT ON STUDIES, ACADEMIC YEAR 1968–69

Mr. David Helfgott

Subject Piano. Professor Cyril Smith: "In many
ways he is, even now, scarcely reliable, never
having his feet placed quite squarely on the
ground, but there have been moments and even
minutes of near genius."

Composition. Mr. Bryan Kelly: "Mr. Helfgott is,
without question, the most frustrating student I
have ever tried to work with. Being totally
undisciplined, incredibly sloppy, and oblivious
to suggestion, he has produced no single, complete meaningful piece of music. Behind his in-
comprehensible (but often delightful) exterior,
there seems to be considerable talent but it is
thoroughly confounded by his approach to
things."

REPORT ON STUDIES, ACADEMIC YEAR
1969–1970

Mr. David Helfgott

Subject Piano. Professor Cyril Smith: "His life has
been so disordered and chaotic that pianistic
progress has only been allowed sporadic oppor-

tunity. Nevertheless, such fantastic hands have sometimes produced almost unbelievably brilliant passages."

Composition/Analysis. Mr. Bryan Kelly: "A calmer approach wanted in work, a very hectic year."

Undoubtedly, David did give some brilliant performances in London. Among these was his rendition of Rachmaninoff's Third Piano Concerto in D Minor in July 1969, for which he was awarded the Dannreuther Prize for best performance of a piano concerto at the Royal College of Music for that year. However, the way it is depicted in *Shine*—as a dramatic scene in which David collapses on stage while playing, causing him to suffer a mental breakdown and then to return directly to Perth—is entirely fictional.

Firstly, David had already played the piece in public several times before, for example, in Perth and Melbourne in 1964. Secondly, David did not collapse. Thirdly, he stayed in London for another year after this performance, giving several other concerts, among them Rachmaninoff's Third Piano Concerto again, on March 24, 1970, at the Duke's Hall at the Royal Academy of Music in Marylebone Road. Fourthly, the onset of his illness was slow, both predating and postdating this concert, and his condition was almost certainly connected with a history of chronic mental illness in the Helfgott family. And fifthly, he did not blame his "daddy."

In the published film script (scene 131) the end of the Rachmaninoff scene reads:

DAVID *sweats, hyperventilating.*

DAVID *(mumbling):* "Did my best, Daddy . . ."

. . . David begins to fall backward—in slow motion, in silence until his head hits the stage. His spectacles fly off. Eyes wide open, he stares at bright swirling lights. Silence.

Cut to overhead lights in:

[Scene 132] Interior Hospital ward. Day time . . .

While Rachmaninoff's Third Piano Concerto is undoubtedly a technically and physically demanding piece, the film's attitude to it is quite ridiculous. In scene 98 David's music tutor Cecil Parkes says to David: "No one's ever been mad enough to attempt the Rach 3," and David replies: "Am I mad enough, Professor? Am I?"

The character of Cecil Parkes was played by the eminent British actor Sir John Gielgud at the age of 91. The figure upon whom Parkes was loosely based is David's music tutor at the Royal College, Cyril Smith. Smith was famous for having the use of only his right hand after suffering a stroke that paralyzed his left. He had become David's tutor as a result of being an acquaintance of Professor Callaway in Perth. Smith was a highly distinguished man. He had been professor of pianoforte at the Royal College since as long ago as 1934, and was acclaimed as a fine interpreter of Rachmaninoff. Sergei Rachmaninoff himself—whom Smith had met on many occasions—said before his death in 1943, that Smith had given the best performance by any Englishman of his Third Piano Concerto.

Smith had risen to stardom from a humble background. He was born the son of a bricklayer, and grew up in a working-class part of Middlesburough, an industrial city in the far north of England known for its shipbuilding. He was a brilliant musician and himself attended the Royal College. But at the age of forty-six, during a concert tour of Russia, disaster struck: he suffered a stroke and lost the use of his left hand. He had been asked by Walter Legge of EMI to record Rachmaninoff's concertos and was in the process of preparing for this when the tragedy prevented it. With remarkable fortitude, he rehabilitated himself, rebuilt his life, and embarked on a new career. He now played three hands on two pianos with his wife Phyllis Sellick, with whom he had previously formed a conventional two-piano team. This experience is recounted in his moving and inspirational autobiography, *Duet for Three Hands.*

Professor Immelman, who, like David, was one of Smith's pupils, told me: "Cyril Smith was a rather shy but also a passionate man and a great teacher. He had a sharp and penetrating mind and brought to his teaching the experience he had gained on the concert platform. He considered instrumental mastery to be vital for any aspiring pianist. But it was only a means to an end, the springboard from which a performance can take off. The firmer the technical base, the greater the flights of true musical imagination can be. From the moment one entered his teaching room all that mattered was the quality of one's playing. He was relentless in his pursuit of productive practicing procedures no matter how unusual or extreme. Those of us who had the privilege to study with him (and we knew ourselves to be privileged) acquired skills of objective analysis that could be applied to all areas of the repertoire even many years later."

Immelman added that "John Gielgud's portrayal of a woolly minded exponent of what I call 'Fjords in Norway' school of piano teaching and the endless ego-tripping could not be further removed from the truth. Far from being a doddery man, Cyril was very sharp."

Smith died in 1974, but in April 1997, his widow, Phyllis Sellick, herself a concert pianist of great ability, phoned me from London after reading an interview with me about *Shine* in a British newspaper. When I mentioned to her that I was considering writing a book, she strongly encouraged me to include what she had to say:

"David did not break down or collapse when playing Rachmaninoff's Third Piano Concerto as depicted in the film. I was at that performance, and it was a wonderful rendition by David . . . During the four years that David was Cyril's pupil, we became friendly and saw him on many occasions outside his lessons. He never once said anything about his father being violent to him. Quite the contrary. They seemed to be very close. David told Cyril and me that he got along very well with his father and that his father had been writing him lots of lovely letters whilst he was in London."

She also complained about the way her husband's character had been portrayed in general throughout

Shine. "Cyril would never have said things like 'Don't you just love those big fat chords' to describe Rachmaninoff's music; or 'the piano is a monster; tame it or it'll swallow you whole!' That's just ridiculous," Phyllis Sellick told me.

David's forty-minute performance of Rachmaninoff's Third Piano Concerto was undoubtedly one of the highlights of his time in England. Mr. J. R. Stainer, registrar of the college, who was present, wrote afterward: "I have not heard a bigger ovation since I have been at the college." And Professor Immelman told a leading British arts television program, *The South Bank Show,* that when David was rehearsing for the Third Piano Concerto, people often dropped into the concert hall to listen. "They knew it was special, but that performance in late July 1969 exceeded everyone's expectations. I find it particularly unfortunate that the memory of this glorious occasion was degraded by the film suggesting, without any justification, that David had suffered a blackout. Nothing like that occurred."

Immelman told me, no doubt exaggerating a little: "For anyone connected with the Royal College in the late sixties, David's performance of the Rachmaninoff Third Piano Concerto has become a point of reference almost along the lines of 'Do you remember where you were when you heard that Kennedy had been shot?' It was one of those rare occasions when everything came together. Of course David had all the virtuoso qualities required for this challenging work but he also had the gift for playing gentle, expressive passages with a freshness and freedom that rendered them pure, almost innocent, so far removed from the tricky self-indulgent approach often encountered. The excellent integration with the orchestra achieved on this occasion also reflected the care and attention to detail that David and Smith had lavished on the score."

Immelman also remembers that "he did do something rather unusual after the Rachmaninoff concert. He was driven back to his modest one-room apartment by an elated Cyril Smith and Phyllis Sellick and as soon as he got home he threw some clothes into a bag and set off for the launderette!"

Throughout 1969 and 1970 David's behavior became more and more unbalanced and his moods swung up and down erratically. Professor Immelman said: "David's behavior was often unusual, a trifle eccentric. Not many of us realized at the time that he was suffering mental problems, but with hindsight one recognizes that there were already signs of chemical imbalance. I certainly do not recall him ever saying anything negative about his father or mentioning his father in this respect."

David's condition worsened to such an extent that in October 1969 he checked into a psychiatric hospital for the first time. He told us in a letter that he was seeking psychiatric treatment, but knowing how distraught Dad would be at the news, he didn't admit at the time that he was actually confined to a hospital. It was all very traumatic for a young boy who had been the subject of so much attention and praise and upon whom so many expectations had been placed only a few years earlier.

11

DESCENT INTO ILLNESS

David's last few months in London were not all bad. Having been discharged from the psychiatric hospital shortly before Christmas, he was soon at the piano again, continuing to practice and perform. He gave another performance of Rachmaninoff's Third Piano Concerto on March 24, 1970, at the Duke's Hall of the Royal Academy of Music (a separate institution from the Royal College). This time around, however, David's playing was far poorer. Cyril Smith is reported to have said after the concert: "I did not teach him to play like that." Roberta Dodds, a Royal College staff member, added that the performance had been "histrionic."

A month later, on April 24, David gave a much better performance. As part of a charity concert, he played Liszt's Piano Concerto No. 1 in E-flat before 8,000 people at the Royal Albert Hall, one of

England's largest classical music concert venues. Critics were eager to praise him once more. One wrote: "David Helfgott completely identified himself with this romantic music, his fabulous technique in the louder passages being equalled by the exquisite poetry of the more lyrical places."

But over the next three months David's condition took a rapid turn for the worse. By the summer he was writing to us of his longing to come home and be with his family again. He began sending letters to the people who had been responsible for organizing his trip to London in the hope that they would provide the financial means for his return.

On July 5, 1970, he wrote to Mrs. Luber-Smith about his "psycho-trouble," explaining how terrible it was and that it wasn't his fault. While the letter was reasonably chatty, and expressed the hope that one day he would get better, he also told her that he could not endure another chilly winter in London without a place to live, and he really wanted to come back to Australia.

Four days later, on July 9, David wrote a far more distraught letter, this time to Professor Callaway. He said that he was simply not able to survive in London any longer. He told Callaway that he had no food, no money, no job, and no accommodation. He pleaded with him to arrange his fare home. On the next day, July 10, no doubt worried that the letter would take too long to arrive, David sent Professor Callaway a cable—this time begging him to be allowed to return to Perth.

On July 13, Professor Callaway's secretary, Lorna Trist, wrote back to David to say that their office had only received his cable that morning and that Callaway was overseas in Moscow and would not get David's message until he returned to Perth the following weekend. Trist let David know that she had immediately passed his frantic message to Mr. Walton, the secretary of the Music Council, who was that very day sending him a banker's draft to help him with his living expenses.

But clearly this wasn't enough for the overwrought David. On July 18, he again wrote to Callaway, asking to come home as soon as possible.

Professor Callaway replied on August 6 and has kindly granted his copyright permission to reprint the letter.

DEPARTMENT OF MUSIC

August 6th, 1970.

Mr. David Helfgott,
6/8 Evelyn Gardens,
LONDON. S.W.7. England.

Dear David,
  I am sorry I have not written before this but, as you are aware, I have been overseas. Unfortunately I did not get to London this time, so missed seeing you. I am aware that you are now keen to come home and I expect that Mr. Walton of the Music Council will be making the necessary arrangements. You will appreciate that the financial aspect of things is not my concern but rather that of the Music Council. When your

plans are made and you know when you will be arriving in Perth do let me know, as I will be keen to do anything I can to help get you established in Australia. There will be difficulties of course, but all artists have to face up to such problems and I only hope that appropriate opportunities will be forthcoming in your home country.

I was very pleased to hear of all your successes at the Royal College of Music and I know how proud Mr. Cyril Smith and Sir Keith Falkner have been of all your achievements.

With best wishes,

Yours sincerely,

Frank Callaway
Professor of Music

One week later—and four years to the day after he had left for London—David was home. His flight from Heathrow was arranged by the University of Western Australia's Music Council, with the help of Mrs. Luber-Smith and the Jewish community. Since we still didn't have a phone and because the travel plans were made in such a hurry, Rabbi Rubin-Zacks of the Perth Hebrew Orthodox Congregation rushed round to our house on August 13 to let my father know that David would be arriving early the next morning.

During David's final months in London, when he was starting to become seriously ill, David had begun saying, for the first time, confusing and contradictory things to Dad in his letters. He would tell him that he loved him with all his heart and that he missed him and the family terribly, but in the very same letter he would suddenly start harking back to the fact that he had not gone to America nine years earlier, after Isaac Stern's visit. He told Dad that he blamed him for this. Consequently, my father was initially apprehensive about David's return, and not completely sure how David would treat him.

My father had also been terribly shocked and upset by these baseless accusations. David did not seem to realize that he was ill—and that his illness had nothing to do with whether or not he had gone to study in America, or indeed whether he had left the house after an argument. What a terrible thing it must be to accept the fact that one is suffering from mental illness. It requires a tremendous will and readiness to take responsibility, and it is so much easier to start blaming a parent—however loving and concerned that parent has been. As David himself repeatedly put it in later years, this is a period during which his life became "foggy and misty and misty and foggy."

Leslie recently took the letters we received from David during his last months in London to a leading psychiatrist in Perth. We could of course see for ourselves that something was amiss just by looking at the erratic punctuation and odd handwriting. The psychiatrist examined the letters, and told Leslie that it was very common for someone undergoing a mental breakdown to blame a member of his family or someone else close to them.

The psychiatrist said: "These letters are in fact loving letters. They would indicate that David loved his father very much. But they also demonstrate a common occurrence in the mentally ill—the factor of 'blame.' And blaming someone is itself part of the illness. The letters also show that Peter Helfgott seemed to have been a loving and caring father."

My father's anxiety was almost unbearable in the hours before David was due home. He paced restlessly up and down. It was bad enough knowing that David was sliding into serious mental illness without having to contend with accusatory letters. To his immense relief, however, on their reunion at home on August 14 everything was fine.

Dad's fears had been unfounded. After David returned home, he expressed only affection for Dad and never showed hostility toward him either in person or in letters to other people. The next time we heard about the idea of David blaming my father was more than twenty years later, during the making of *Shine*. In 1970, he was just glad to be back in the family nest. He had left London for home so dazed and disorganized that all he brought with him were some odd items of clothing and a few letters and sheets of music. He had forgotten to pack such valuable items as the medal he had been awarded.

I was living in Melbourne at this time and had been receiving daily bulletins from my father, keeping me informed of developments. He wrote to me immediately letting me know of his relief. He told me that as soon as David had arrived home he had "changed his attitude completely and was very grateful for everything" and how "happy everybody was."

My whole family was so overjoyed at David's return that they all wrote to me separately telling me the good news in their own words. Louise, then 10, had been just six years old when David had left for London, so for her it was like receiving a "new" brother. She wrote to me on August 16:

Dear Marg,

On Friday morning at 3.00 A.M. David arrived from London. Rabbi Rubin-Zacks came and told us. On Friday afternoon the rabbi brought David here. David has been living with us ever since. I was surprised when I first saw David as he is fair haired! . . . He has a fabulous technique and I have been getting on very well with him.

(signed off with over 30 kisses)

From the first day David arrived back home, he made it clear that he, too, was overjoyed. It was a world away from the mental distress, loneliness, rain, cold, and lack of food that he had been enduring in London just a few days earlier. His change in mood, said my mother, was miraculous—he even took Suzie, now seventeen, to a concert three days later. He started playing the piano again and went to see Madame Carrard, who he said he had also missed terribly.

He also wrote a very optimistic letter to Professor Callaway, thanking him for helping to arrange the years of study in London, and asking him to convey his thanks to Mr. Walton and the Music Council for assisting him. David let Callaway know he was living back at home with his parents and added that he hoped to be completely well again soon.

But it was not to be. David's condition deteriorated again rapidly. On August 24, only ten days after his return, my father wrote to tell me that David seemed to get exhausted very easily. I was extremely worried about him, not only on account of his health, but also because of his dashed hopes—he had departed for London with such high expectations and dreams of becoming a world-famous pianist, and now he had been compelled to come back unwell and in such haste. I was also anxious about my father because I knew how distressed he was about David. This stress, I knew, was liable to play havoc with my father's health—whenever he worried too much, it caused him heart problems.

I knew that my father was now very concerned that his son might be suffering from the same mental illness that had afflicted both his aunt in Poland and also his beloved sister Hannah. Hannah was the only one of my father's six brothers and sisters to have been spared extermination at the hands of the Nazis. With the outbreak of war imminent, my father had sent all the money he could raise to his father, urging his family to leave Poland. My grandfather had known that of all his children, his fragile daughter Hannah would least be able to stand up to the Nazi terror, and in 1938, my grandfather sent Hannah to join my father in Australia.

My father looked after Hannah, his gentle blond-haired sister, devotedly. But her illness became so severe that she finally had to be institutionalized in Melbourne. Before her condition worsened, she briefly married and had a son, Joe, born in 1949. But two years later, she had to be admitted to hospital, and Joe came to live with us in Melbourne for six months. I remember how my mother used to tend lovingly to him in his cot.

Hannah spent the rest of her life in mental institutions, first in a hospital and then in a hostel for the mentally ill, until her death in 1989, while Joe was raised in an orphanage. Whenever I was in Melbourne I visited Hannah often. I always found her timid, withdrawn, a lost soul. It was often difficult to have a proper conversation with her and sometimes she didn't recognize me at all. My father also visited both Hannah and Joe whenever he could.

My father, it seemed, was once again destined to undergo the anguish of having one of his loved ones afflicted with mental illness. David's condition changed from one day to the next. Sometimes he seemed just fine and played the piano merrily, at others he was utterly drained and exhausted and had to rest frequently.

It was Madame Carrard who suggested David should go for a complete medical checkup. When he did this, at the Sir Charles Gairdner Hospital, in late August, the doctors diagnosed his condition as serious. (The medical records are confidential and cannot be made public unless David gives his permission in writing, which he has always said would be too emotionally traumatic for him.) What we had thought would be a brief examination turned into a prolonged stay and David was in and out of the Sir Charles Gairdner Hospital for the next four and a half months.

(Australia, like many other countries, has a system of free public health care.)

My father immediately wrote to me in Melbourne. "David has entered the hospital," he reported, "and is going to have a complete checkup and the doctor told me he may be there for up to a month." He signed the letter, "Yours always and always, your loving pop forever," with about twenty kisses.

The hospital is on the other side of Perth, and my family visited David at least two or three times every week. My parents didn't own a car and had to make the journey by bus, which took about an hour each way. Dad especially spent as much time as he could visiting David.

David was, on occasion, sedated by the drugs; seeing his son in such a condition broke my father's heart. On September 7, he wrote to me, saying that "I would like to know whether they can trace the root of David's trouble. He's definitely sick. I think it is a biochemical disorder in his organism, and it would affect his behavior in a certain way. I don't like to describe his symptoms in the letter yet, as I like to have the doctor's opinion first."

My father's amateur diagnosis was later proved correct by medical experts. David suffers from a biochemical disorder, which is a physical condition in the same way that diabetes or a liver complaint are physical conditions. He is not, as Gillian so blithely suggests, merely "a delightful eccentric." He was diagnosed with schizo-affective disorder, which can produce the symptoms of both schizophrenia and/or mood disorder.

Naturally, I was extremely worried about my darling brother, imagining him to be in a terrible state. I pictured scenes of the kind in movies where mental hospitals are shown as hideous, scary places. So it came as a great relief to me when my family wrote to tell me that the Sir Charles Gairdner Hospital was not like that at all and that David was in fact quite cheerful, sitting up in bed and asking for an astronomy book to read.

I even cried when I received a sweet letter from him (dated September 11) confirming that he really was in an upbeat mood. He told me in the letter that the hospital was "very nice," how happy he was that all the family were coming to visit him and that everything was fine. He said Madame Carrard had promised to give him lessons again shortly and that he was looking forward to playing duets and concertos with me soon.

The psychiatric wing was part of the general hospital. The gardens were beautifully kept, and the devoted staff had done their best to make the wards light and pleasant. David wasn't usually heavily medicated at that time—that came some years later when he was in another Perth hospital, Graylands, and it was most distressing to witness.

My family wrote to me about the atmosphere in the hospital, which was friendly and—as far as possible—relaxed. David was in Block C, a newly built wing. My parents and siblings described in their letters how the nurses hovered around David, and how cheerful he was, especially on the days my parents came to visit. His ward was colorfully painted with artworks displayed on the walls and there were always flowers.

Leslie also paid him frequent visits, and the two of them even managed to find a table-tennis table to play on in the hospital recreation room. In fact, there was a wealth of activities laid on for the patients, including handicrafts, volley ball, and lawn bowls on the grass outside. The hospital even organized cricket matches between the staff and the patients. Individual counseling and group therapy were also available. There was a TV lounge, too. David also went on the walks the staff organized in nearby King's Park, the area of natural bush land that we had loved going to as children.

Conditions for David in the hospital have been depicted as harsh and gloomy in much of the material that has been written about him as a result of *Shine*. Media reports have suggested that David had a terrible time locked up and languishing in mental institutions. In fact, the Sir Charles Gairdner Hospital was a very stimulating environment. Leslie remembers hearing one patient there comment that it was more like a hotel than a hospital.

After the first few weeks of hospitalization, David was allowed to come and go freely, and he often visited the family. When he was at home, he would practice the piano again. At one point, Professor Callaway even arranged a series of concerts for David through the University of Western Australia Music Department. David played on two occasions, but the remaining concerts had to be canceled because of his illness.

It was also while he was in the Sir Charles Gairdner Hospital that David started going swimming every day. He would go down to the beach, no matter what the weather. (In London, he had not always been able to afford the entrance charges to public swimming pools, so he had gone for dips in the murky waters of the Serpentine Lake in Hyde Park.) Since that time, David's enjoyment of swimming has turned into an obsession, which has never abated.

My father's grief at having to come to terms with another member of his close family succumbing to mental illness was modified at least in part by the knowledge that David, although undoubtedly sick, was being well cared for and was not too unhappy.

Professor Callaway, who has only ever wanted the best for my brother, says that it was during this period of hospitalization that he realized that sending David to London may have been a mistake. "It's a great pity that Scott Hicks did not consult with me over *Shine*," he told me. "I would have told him that I now realize in retrospect, given David's breakdown, that it would have been a good idea to have consulted more fully with Peter Helfgott about the suitability of David's going to London. As it is, *Shine*—although in some respects a remarkable film—turned out to be far from the truth."

Of the failure to consult David's music teacher, Madame Carrard, about David's trip, Callaway says: "This was not my decision. The Music Council of the university were the decision-makers, not myself."

The way in which David's return from London is portrayed in *Shine* is utterly false, and could even be called cruel. It is another key element in building up a ghastly, totally distorted picture of my father and David's relationship with him.

In *Shine,* the following two scenes occur straight after David's collapse while playing the "Rach 3" (scene 131):

SCENE 132 INTERIOR. HOSPITAL WARD. DAY-TIME

DAVID's glasses are put on a metal tray. Electrodes are placed on his temples. The ECT dial is turned up. DAVID's fingers flutter as the current runs through his body and then they quiver to a stop. He lies there, staring into a void of white light. The phone keeps ringing.

Cut to close-up—the phone still ringing. A hand picks up the receiver.

MAN: Hello. (No response) Hello, who is this?

The accent strikes us—it is PETER. *We are in:*

SCENE 133 INTERIOR. HELFGOTT HOUSE. NIGHT

PETER: Hello?

DAVID: Hello, Daddy?

SCENE 134 INTERIOR. PHONE BOOTH. DAY

DAVID, *hair cut short, pale and gaunt, clutches his bag.*

DAVID: Daddy? I'm back.

SCENE 135 RESUME—*Peter, numb. He listens in silence, then hangs up slowly. New angle seen through the window:* PETER *stands there, stunned. He pulls the blind down. Fade to black.*

In the next scene we are back in what the screenplay describes as "the morning sun" in the psychiatric hospital gardens. The way *Shine* shows David being shunned by his family on his return to Perth is a lie from start to finish—beginning with the fact that David did not receive ECT shock treatment at this time. Nor did we own a telephone. And, as at many other points in the film, it is remarkable that my father is always shown in the dark, as though we did not own any lightbulbs at home, whereas phone booths and even psychiatric hospitals are by comparison bathed in light.

Even more outrageous is what Gillian writes in *Love You to Bits and Pieces:* "Peter Helfgott came to visit David during his first week in hospital . . . After being told that there was nothing physically wrong with David, Peter never came to see him in the hospital again . . . Peter went home in a rage . . . He [found] a suitcase of his son's private possessions—forwarded by a London friend shortly after David had returned—and among these things Peter found a little bundle of Katherine Susannah Pritchard's* letters.

---

*Pritchard was a founding member of the Australian Communist Party and music lover, whom David had befriended prior to going to London, but had passed away while he was there.

'Father burned them all,' David recalled. 'It was done very surreptitiously, it was done very brilliantly. It was out of spite.' . . . Bewildered by Peter's perverse act, David hardly saw his father or any family over the next three years."

David was discharged from the hospital on January 16, 1971. After this, my brother's life took a decided turn for the better as a wonderful woman entered into it.

12

A FIRST MARRIAGE:
THE STORY OF CLAIRE

On June 26, 1971, less than six months after he had been discharged from the psychiatric hospital, David again won the State Final of the ABC Concerto and Vocal Competition. His performance of Rachmaninoff's "Rhapsody on a Theme by Paganini," with the West Australian Symphony Orchestra under the baton of conductor Tibor Paul, "electrified the capacity audience," reported the Perth *Sunday Times* the following morning. His victory was "a unanimous decision," said the paper. The judges who had been enthralled by his playing did not know that my brother had also been enraptured: his "electric" performance was sparked by his meeting a few months earlier with the woman who, two weeks later, on July 10, would become his wife. David knew that his startlingly swift rehabilitation was largely due to one person: Claire.

"I have never seen a man more in love with a woman than David was with Claire," their friend and neighbor at the time, Allan Macpherson, told me recently.

Though he was fairly upbeat when discharged from the hospital, five months in a psychiatric ward had inevitably taken a toll on David. The improvement in his mood in the six months that followed was partly the result of the love and care that my parents had given him, and also due to assistance from others—in particular, Cliff Harris, president of the Music Council and a Perth City councilor. Harris organized a grant for David from the Perth mayor's office, enabling him to be set up in a flat of his own and provided with a piano. But above all David's astonishing recovery was the result of his relationship with Claire.

David had been introduced to her by Carl Berent early in February 1971, about three weeks after he left the hospital. Both Claire and Carl were members of the "Cultural Club," a small local group of music and arts enthusiasts. My brother and I had known Carl since childhood. Carl was a piano teacher who also played with several orchestras in Perth. He had been a friend of my father and had given us a few piano lessons before we started with Frank Arndt. Carl could see instantly how much David liked Claire, a widow several years older than David who was bringing up four young children. Carl wanted to help David, realizing that he was somewhat disoriented after his discharge from the hospital. Knowing how warm and giving Claire was, he encouraged her to get to know David better (as did Madame Carrard). After their first meeting, David told Carl how very much he wanted to see the pretty, dark-haired woman again.

Claire told me: "David and I quickly struck up a friendship. David started to visit me often. He was a gentle person and we shared a love of music and had a lot of fun together. After a while our friendship developed into a relationship. He wanted to stay with me more and more, which I didn't mind at all since he got on very well with my children. He would practice on my piano for hours. I knew how difficult the previous few months had been for him and that he was still under medical treatment and I wanted to do what I could to help.

"Within a short time of moving in, David began telling me how much he loved me and that he wanted to marry me. I didn't take him seriously at first—I didn't really want to marry anyone, and in any case I was not entirely sure about his mental state. But then David started going round telling everyone he was going to marry me, and I realized he was deadly serious."

Before Claire decided whether to accept David's proposal, she thought it a good idea to ask David's doctor, Dr. Czillag, for his opinion. Dr. Czillag headed the Sir Charles Gairdner Psychiatric Unit and, like both Claire and Madame Carrard, was a Hungarian-born Jew. During the months before their marriage, as Claire had grown closer to David, she had come to know his doctors well; indeed, they enlisted her help in ensuring that David took his medication and in monitoring his moods.

Dr. Czillag told Claire that he knew from David how much he loved her and that he believed that the stability of marriage would be excellent for his well-being. He added that David had told him that he had always liked the company of older women because they gave him more sympathy and understanding.

This was not the first time David had fallen for an older woman. While in London he had a relationship with a nurse fifteen years his senior—she had even wanted to follow David back to Australia, but he was too distraught at the time to invite her. Gillian, too, is sixteen years older. The attraction of the older woman probably stems from the fact that David likes and needs a lot of looking after. Older women may express maternal feelings for him whereas younger ones may not have the necessary patience or maturity.

"Dr. Czillag told me there was another pressing reason, too," Claire added. "He said he was very worried about the harm that interfering busybodies were continuing to cause David. He said he could not believe the audacity of people like Mrs. Luber-Smith, Cliff and Rae Harris, and the conductor Georg Tintner. They were still trying to take control of David and push him toward being a world-class concert pianist without any regard for the medical consequences.

"Dr. Czillag said the Harrises were trying to raise money to send David away again to study, this time to America, and an announcement about this had again appeared in the paper. He stressed that David simply would not be able to handle the pressure of going abroad. He needed rest and stability. Marriage, he said, would have the benefit of serving as a kind of protection for David, since he could see that Claire had his best interests at heart. 'It's the people who are interfering in David's life that are aggravating his condition,' Dr. Czillag said."

Claire told me that she could see for herself how these people were trying to influence and manipulate David against his family, even after he had returned from London. "They were trying to persuade him that it was they who wanted what was best for him," she said, adding, "Peter was a bit of a softie and could not stand up to these people. His manner was too gentle for a confrontation."

David's other doctor, Dr. Matthews, was equally angry with the people interfering in David's life, and he, too, stressed the need for love and stability. Claire told me: "Of course I said yes out of love, but it reassured me that his doctors thought it was a good idea. They also led me to believe that David's illness could be controlled and that further hospitalization would not be necessary. I don't think I've ever seen David look happier than when I said 'yes.'"

Mrs. Luber-Smith's attitude was very different. "David's decision to marry was foolish," she said. "I had nothing to do with David after that. I was so upset that he had left the Harrises after all they had done for him, I just couldn't get involved any further."

Claire and David married in Brisbane Street Synagogue. It was an orthodox service conducted by Rabbi Shalom Coleman. "David and I discussed it and we both decided we wanted a traditional Jewish wedding, albeit a simple and quiet one," said Claire.

Claire had been married before, in 1952 to a fellow Hungarian Jew whom she had met in Perth. But her husband had died of cancer in 1960, leaving her with four small children, who she struggled to bring up on her own. Claire, a cooking teacher by profession, was born in Budapest to a middle-class professional family. Her father had been a textile designer and her mother a schoolteacher.

Her life had included the worst that "humanity" has to offer. Deported as a child by the Germans and their fascist Hungarian allies to the infamous concentration camp at Dachau for the "crime" of being Jewish, she had miraculously survived and emigrated to Australia in 1952.

When American forces entered Dachau on April 29, 1945, what they found—skeletal tortured bodies mangled together, piled naked on top of one another, wriggling and squirming half alive, half dead—was so horrific that, according to a leading Holocaust historian, Sir Martin Gilbert, photographs taken that day have never been published.

"I was liberated by the Americans in May 1945 at the end of the war, in Schwandorf forest," Claire told me, still trembling at the memory. "As the Allies advanced, the Germans had emptied some of the camps, including Dachau. Though they knew the war was lost, they still planned to kill us. Those of us still alive were forced to march to the nearby forest, where it would be easier to bury and hide our bodies. Many thousands of us were gathered there—not just from Dachau but from other camps, too. We had to dig a huge mass grave. The killing went on all night. But then the SS heard the approach of tanks from far away, and fled. When the tanks arrived, American soldiers jumped out and hugged and kissed us children. We were petrified, starving, and itching, because we were covered in lice. A black American soldier took me in his arms and started crying."

Claire, who was fourteen at the time of the liberation, was left with no parents, aunts, or grandparents, and was subsequently looked after by an American Jewish organization. She went to a school for Jewish orphans run by the Americans in Germany. (At the time, the British were still using all means necessary to prevent Jewish Holocaust survivor children from entering Palestine.) "Eventually I chose to go to Australia. I imagined it to be a place with no guns, no war," Claire told me. "The United Nations relief agency arranged my flight." (Though Australia, like most countries, was very restrictive in the number of Jews it agreed to admit immediately before the war, it was much more generous in allowing Jewish survivors to move there after the war, as part of its enlarged immigrant intake from all over Europe.)

At the time of David and Claire's wedding, which happened at short notice, I was living in Melbourne and unfortunately wasn't able to take time off work to make the long journey back. We still didn't own a phone, but my father had written immediately to let me know the good news.

I returned to Perth the following month, and, of course, I couldn't wait to meet Claire. I had heard so many good things about her, and I knew she had had a wonderful influence on David. Claire and I quickly became friends, a friendship that has lasted to this day. I regard her and her children as extended family. I have always admired her, not just for her warmth, courage, and sincerity, but for her commitment to David—especially considering how difficult life with him could sometimes be. His health went through frequent bad patches, and she would update me, his concerned older sister, on his condition.

Claire said recently: "My relationship with all of David's family was an excellent one. I could see how close they were, which I liked since I had come from a very close family myself. David had taken me to visit his parents a few times before we were married. His father always welcomed him by putting his arm around him. After the first time we visited, David was very happy because, he said, "My mom and dad liked you very much."

"Peter and Rae often came to visit us. Peter was kind and good-natured. We used to chat about life in Eastern Europe. My children all liked him very much—he told them jokes and stories from the circus and played the violin for my daughter, who also became friendly with David's youngest sister Louise."

Claire was stunned by what she saw in *Shine:* "During the whole time that I was with him, David never once told me that his father had beaten him or ill-treated him in any way. He always talked about his father with love. He told me how lonely he had felt in England, and how many times he had thought to himself that perhaps he should never have left. He told me that it was at those times that he realized how wrong it would have been if he had gone alone to America after Isaac Stern's visit."

There is no sense in which David was "lying dying on the floors of halfway houses" after his return from London, as Scott Hicks claimed at the official pre-Oscar press conference in Los Angeles. Nor was his life devoid of music until Gillian "rescued" him.

Throughout the 1970s and 1980s David spent a great deal of time at the piano and gave many concerts, especially during the period when he was under Claire's solicitous eye.

Allan Macpherson, a former classical music radio producer who knew both David and Claire very well throughout this time, recalls: "In his first year with Claire, David's playing and mental condition improved. Claire asked Carl Berent, who had successfully trained two State winners in the ABC Concerto and Vocal Competition, to train David. David liked Carl and felt comfortable with him. Carl was fully aware of David's mental condition and could communicate with him better than anyone else I knew."

At the time he met Claire, according to Macpherson, David could play long and difficult pieces but lacked finesse. The first thing Carl persuaded him to do was to slow his playing down, in some cases to half speed, as David tended to race his pieces and bravura passages. He also transformed David's somewhat "bashy" sound into a more sophisticated tone. He worked with him to prepare a recital of solo pieces, improving David's keyboard technique as well as his conceptual approach to music; and he inculcated the romance, drama, and tragedy that the pieces required. They worked together on "Pictures at an Exhibition" by Mussorgsky, the Sonata in B Minor by Liszt, "Gaspard de la Nuit" by Ravel, "L'Isle Joyeuse" by Debussy, the "Appassionata" Sonata by Beethoven, and the Ballade in G Minor and Polonaise in E Minor by Chopin.

Macpherson was intimately involved in classical musical circles in Western Australia at the time and

wrote regularly on classical music for various magazines. "David was quite remarkable to hear," he recalls. "He played powerfully and managed difficult
bravura passages with great dexterity and accuracy.
He was in excellent physical condition. I remember
that he had broad shoulders and that his back mus-
cles rippled through his shirt when he played. There
was no sign of the hunchback or disabled demeanor
he was to develop later.

"He was friendly, even ingratiating, but mostly
shy," Macpherson continues. "His only eccentricities
were noisy breathing and face-pulling while he performed. He kept his face very close to the keyboard
and sometimes muttered along with the music as he
played. When I helped him and Carl by turning the
pages David spoke little but frequently said 'yes, yes,
yes.' David was different. My first impression of him
was that he was an inhabitant of another place, another world. Everyone made a tremendous fuss of
him and I am sure that he enjoyed the attention."

In 1972, David's mental condition again took a turn
for the worse. He became morose and languid,
stopped exercising, and even gave up playing the
piano for several weeks. That year he failed to qual-
ify for the ABC Concerto and Vocal Competition,
which greatly upset him. "Claire tried to do everything for him—she even negotiated with the ABC to
enable David to give broadcasts of piano works, but
his playing was so poor and he was so uncommu-
nicative that they abandoned the project," says
Macpherson.

With Carl and Claire's help, however, David's playing improved again. In July 1973 he gave a triumphant

performance of Shostakovich's Concerto for Piano, Trumpet and Strings with the West Australian Symphony Orchestra. Under the heading "Pianist Dazzles at Concert," the music critic of *The West Australian* newspaper, Mary Tannock, gave it a glowing report: "Local pianist David Helfgott stole the show at the Perth Concert Hall last night . . . Mr Helfgott gave a dazzling display. He brilliantly juxtaposed frenzied clarity in the first movement with even-tempered expressiveness in the second. The detail and momentum of the entire interpretation was superb."

But as is often the case with people suffering from schizo-affective disorder, David's condition gradually grew worse. Living with him, admits Claire, could be very difficult. Allan Macpherson recalls that "when David reentered the ABC competition a year later and was not even placed, he cried and muttered so much that Claire had to get the paramedics to help get him home. Claire's effort in looking after David was nothing short of superhuman. She cared for David a great deal, and looked after him continuously without any support from outside agencies. She became a focus of love for him, a kind of whole world, just like the piano. Claire was only a small woman and David almost engulfed her. He would lock his arms around her shoulders and continually kiss her on the cheek, stroke her arms, and fondle her clothing. He would behave like this in company, which I think became embarrassing for Claire. When he was not touching her, he would stare at her transfixed as if experiencing a religious vision."

Claire now says that in spite of his condition at that time, David was nevertheless far better then than he is now. "You could conduct a proper conversation with him and his piano playing was also better. He did not smoke or drink lots of tea or coffee; and he did not kiss or hug or touch people, including almost total strangers, to the extent he does now."

In 1974, things continued to decline and David's behavior grew more erratic. Claire remembers that he would physically cling to her and when she had to go to give cooking lessons, she always wondered where he would be when she got home. Sometimes, he would spend hours practicing, but at other times he would run to the beach, a couple of miles away, and swim for hours. Once she had to fetch the lifeguards to bring him back to shore because he just wouldn't get out of the water.

One day, after searching everywhere for David, Claire discovered that he had admitted himself to Graylands Psychiatric Hospital. "He had done so without telling me first. I was extremely upset. I had realized that he would never fully recover, but I thought that with treatment his illness could be controlled without the need for further hospitalization. I went to see him every day. Peter and other family members were always there. I sat with him for hours and also often phoned. David told me over and over again that the pianist Horowitz had been in a mental hospital and had come out healthy and playing again. 'It doesn't matter if I am a bit different,' he said, 'I'll be okay.'"

Naturally, this was a terrible time for the entire Helfgott family. I visited David frequently. It was very upsetting for us to see him so heavily medicated and looking so distraught.

When David was allowed to leave the hospital in April 1975, he decided to move back into the family home, explaining to Claire that his family could devote all their attention to him, whereas she had her own children to care for. Claire said: "As much as he said he needed me and loved me, he needed the warmth of his parents even more."

In the meantime, David had fallen in love with another woman, whom he had met in the hospital. Claire and David saw less and less of each other, and eventually divorced. Claire recalls, "At that time I thought it better to stay away from David as there was not much more I could do for him under the circumstances."

Scott Hicks chose to leave Claire out of *Shine* altogether. One reason for this may be that including her would have altered the impression that Gillian was David's savior, and that David probably remained a virgin into middle age. In the film Gillian injects love, music, and light into what is depicted as David's otherwise gray and miserable world; then toward the end of the story, they are shown having sex.

But perhaps the real reason for leaving Claire out was that even Hicks could not quite stomach the things that Gillian had to say about her. Of the many cruel, spiteful things included by Gillian in her book, perhaps the most unpardonable is what is written about Claire. Referring to her by her Hungarian name, Clara, Claire is described as "the world's greatest bitch." Gillian quotes David as saying that marrying Claire was "the greatest mistake of his life" and that their marriage was "made in hell and consecrated by and presided over by the Devil." She writes that Claire "would publicly ridicule and bully" David and that "David shivered at the memory" of Claire.

Just in case we miss the point, Gillian has entitled the chapter about Claire "Made in Hell," but opens it with a line about herself: "David was totally *'joyeux'* about my decision to marry him."

Not surprisingly, Claire is distraught by what has been written about her. In its first few months Gillian's book sold an astonishing 60,000 copies in Australia alone and was high up on the best-seller lists in the United States and several other countries. Claire told me that as a result she has suffered enormous distress and all kinds of medical problems. She asked the publisher to remove the sections referring to her from the book, as well as demanding an apology from Gillian. Both requests have been refused. (At least four other people, including myself, have written to the Australian publisher, Penguin, to complain about the way we are portrayed in Gillian's book. I have also agreed to honor Claire's request not to reveal her last name as she has already received more than enough harassment from the press and others as a result of Gillian's book.)

"David's mind has been poisoned against me by Gillian," says Claire. "What she quotes David as saying is pure fabrication and fantasy. She has simply put the words into his mouth. It's very easy to get David to agree to anything. He would mimic everything put to him. As for the 'factual' claims in Gillian's book, such as the one that I sold David's piano in order to make some money for myself, these are too ludicrous

(From cover) Margaret with David at his
beloved piano in August 1996.
(MELVYN TUCKEY)

Peter Elias Helfgott, probably on his way
back into Poland to see his family again.

Rae, my mother *(on the right)*, in 1936
in Czestochowa, Poland, at age 16.

Rae and Peter Helfgott just after their
engagement, in Melbourne.
(MIRIAM LEMISH)

Rae and Peter Helfgott on their wedding day in Melbourne, 1944. *Back row, left to right:* Mrs. Stark, David Granek, Peter Helfgott, Morry Granek, Mrs. Lew. *Front row:* Rebecca Granek, Esther Lew, Rae Helfgott, Miram Stark, Shirley Lew.

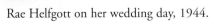

Rae Helfgott on her wedding day, 1944.

Peter and Rae Helfgott with Margaret in 1945

Photo of Peter Helfgott's sister Hannah Helfgott and her passport documentation. She also suffered from mental illness and was hospitalized for most of her life.
(MARGARET HELFGOTT)

David at 12.

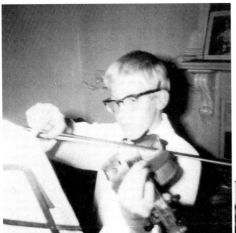

My brother Leslie practicing on his violin, at age 10 or 11, in Perth.

Margaret Helfgott, practicing for the Concerto & Vocal competition in Perth, 1967.
(WEST AUSTRALIAN NEWSPAPERS)

The family in Highgate, 1960. *Back row, from left:* David, Rae with baby Louise, and Margaret. *Front row:* Suzie and Leslie. (PETER HELFGOTT)

Margaret at 15, with David, 13, in the back yard of our home in Perth, 1961. (PETER HELFGOTT)

Peter giving the young David a lesson. David was enraptured with the piano from the moment he could touch the keys. David wrote a tribute to his father in the newspaper after he died. (MARGARET HELFGOTT)

My parents outside Perth Zoo in 1962 (MARGARET HELFGOTT)

Peter Helfgott's three-wheeler motor bike, on which he used to take the Helfgott children for hair-raising rides. (PETER HELFGOTT)

Margaret with Frank Arndt in Perth, 1996.

David's piano teacher, Madame Alice Carrard, aged 97, and Margaret Helfgott, in 1994.

A photo taken of the musical Helfgott family to mark Margaret's appearance in the state finals of the Concerto & Vocal competition in Perth, 1967. *Back row, from left:* Peter, Margaret, Rae; *front row:* Suzie, Louise, Leslie. (David was studying in London at the time.) The portrait of Margaret on the piano was done by Mrs. Adela Shaw of Melbourne, an artist friend of Rae and Peter Helfgott.

David at 14, with his favorite black cat at his feet at our home in Perth, 1961. (MARGARET HELFGOTT)

David and Margaret, playing a two-piano work at Dorothy Croft's house, 1980. (RAE HELFGOTT)

Leslie *(on violin)* and David *(on piano)* with Mom, and David's close friend Dorothy Croft, 1980.

David with Reverend Robert Fairman at Gildercliffe Lodge, 1982.

Rae Helfgott in 1980.
(Margaret Helfgott)

Rae Helfgott with *(left to right)* my brothers and sisters David, Leslie, Louise and Suzie, 1975. David was living happily at home with his parents at this time, after coming out of the hospital. Peter Helfgott was nursing him full-time.
(Margaret Helfgott)

Peter Helfgott's grave site, with the stone the Helfgott family had inscribed "In Loving Memory."

David and his teacher, Hungarian-born Madame Alice Carrard, the grand old lady of Perth's musical circles, in approximately 1985.

Leslie playing violin with David in 1990, straight out of the swimming pool. David goes swimming almost every day, whatever the weather. In January 1988, he was proud to play at the opening of the World Swimming Championships.

David and Les in a serious political discussion, 1996.
(MELVYN TUCKEY)

Margaret Helfgott on her wedding day in Jerusalem, with her mother, Rae Helfgott, who flew in from Australia for the occasion, 1988.
(DOREEN KAHILLA)

to be dignified with a reply. I think everyone can see who is making the money."

Macpherson told me that the claim made in Gillian's book that Claire married with a view to making money out of David's career is preposterous. David did not earn money and was a complete financial burden to Claire throughout their marriage. Her eldest son had to find a job to help out because David wasn't earning anything.

Claire has already suffered more at the hands of the Nazis than most of us are ever likely to endure. It is impossible adequately to express how upset my family and I are at the association of words like "hell" and "devil" with my former sister-in-law, one of the kindest and most decent people I have ever met. "It is just outrageous," says my brother Leslie.

To all those who know Claire, Gillian's remarks would be laughable, were they not so cruel. That Claire is an extremely generous person can be seen, for example, by the fact that she shared her home for three years with a runaway Aboriginal girl who was desperate not to return to the orphanage from which she had escaped. Another Aboriginal girl, who was blind from birth and lives in an institution, comes to stay with Claire every weekend.

Even today, in spite of what David says—or is made to say—in *Love You to Bits and Pieces,* Claire tells me of her concern for David's welfare whenever we speak. As far as his current fame is concerned, she says "for David's sake, I'm happy that he believes that he has made it, but I'm sad at the way he has been exploited."

I received a lovely letter from Claire's eldest son Ray after *Shine* came out.

"Dear Margaret," he wrote. "It is unbelievable the way that your father has been portrayed, particularly in the film. I recall meeting him on a number of occasions including when he visited our home. He was nothing like the person he is now being presented as by Gillian and others. His concern for the family always came through and I found his manner to be unassuming and gentlemanly. . . . I know how difficult David could be, particularly as his condition deteriorated. However, I was always impressed by the way his family stood by him and tried to help. Then as now, it was very easy for everybody to offer advice and criticize, but when it actually came to helping David through his difficult periods those same people would not be there. Unfortunately, David's talent attracted people to him in the way in which many people wish to be associated with success or apparent success.

"I clearly recall the love and care your father and family had for David, no matter what, so can empathize with the suffering created by the absolute distortion that has been presented about your father and the family in general. It is very sad that such a circus has been created around David and to me the motives are obvious. However, doing it by walking over the memory of a decent person such as your father is unforgivable. I can clearly understand, because the absolute garbage that Gillian has written about my mother has deeply upset me, too."

I find these words heartwarming. I also feel that it is Allan Macpherson, who knew David and Claire intimately, who gives an accurate summary of the whole situation. In his words: "At the time, it was very sad to see them going through what was a massive struggle. But it is even sadder today that David recollects—through the opinions of his second wife—that his life with Claire was such a misery. The truth is that if there was any misery then it was indisputably attributable to his own condition and illness. Life with Claire was never "hell" for David. He was extremely fortunate that he had someone so considerate and responsible to look after him."

13

MY FATHER'S FINAL YEARS

When David left Graylands Hospital and moved back home in April 1975, my father was seventy-one and six years into his retirement. Heartbroken to see David in such a sad condition, Dad dedicated the rest of his life to helping his son.

Looking after David was a great strain on the family. While the mentally ill suffer great pain, the impact on their family and those around them is often forgotten, even though they are in effect the secondary victims of mental illness. David could be extremely difficult. For example, he made Dad send all his clothes to the dry cleaners, which would cost my father a small fortune. He also insisted that he be allowed to practice the piano whenever he liked, even in the middle of the night. My father acquiesced to almost all of David's wishes. He was still in excellent physical shape despite his heart and chest problems, and would often hop on the back of Leslie's motorbike and go off and run errands for David. David's eating habits were also prone to radical change. On some days, he would eat nothing at all, while there were other periods where he gorged himself and became quite overweight. At one stage he grew a beard, and on occasion he stooped over like a hunchback.

Dad was always looking for ways to stimulate David. He thought that learning something new would be good therapy, and asked David if he would like to play the violin. David was very enthusiastic. "He was an extremely fast learner; he had perfect pitch," recalls Leslie, the violinist in the family, who helped my father teach David this new skill. Despite his poor health, David was very ambitious. After only a few lessons he was attempting to tackle some of the more difficult violin concertos, such as the Tchaikovsky Concerto, although getting through such demanding works was a struggle. David also liked accompanying Leslie's violin playing at the piano. Leslie had reached a high level of proficiency, passing his seventh-grade practical violin music exams.

By now our whole house was filled with music. There were two pianos, four violins, bongo drums, a xylophone, and a chromatic harmonica—all of which my father had taught himself to play. Most of all, in his retirement Peter finally had time to play his beloved piano to his heart's content. He would spend up to five hours a day practicing intricate pieces by Chopin, Liszt, and others.

Although his fingers had hardened and become stiff after a lifetime of manual work, my father was able to negotiate the difficult passages and accomplish all sorts of wonders at the keyboard. He also had more time to compose music for the piano. "Have you heard this melody before?" he would often ask me, concerned that he had unintentionally appropriated another composer's work. I would reassure him that he had not. David, like me, was very impressed by Dad's ability as a composer. I still have the letters that David wrote to me in Israel after Dad's death; for example, in the one of February 4, 1976, he praises Dad's talents as a composer and tells me he was planning to "record Dad's fabulous compositions for the ABC." And in his letter of April 2, 1976, David says: "Dad produced some beaut [sic] compositions before he died."

Among other things, my father used his music to express his love for his adopted country. In 1973, Australia decided that it had finally had enough of the British national anthem "God Save the Queen," which Australia had retained even though it had been independent since 1901. Seventy-odd years later someone decided that it was time Australia had an anthem of its own. So a competition was held to choose a new national anthem, and my father was one of the 2,500 Australians to submit an entry. The anthem he wrote went as follows:

"Australia—my wonder land"
 by E.P. Helfgott

Verse 1   Verse 2

A long long time   Work and sweat
Our nation to be   All the way

Ever and ever
We shall be free

Courage and spirit
We possess
Marching forward
To progress

Open spaces
Bright skies
Pleasant sunshine
Nature nice

We build and plough
Our fields
Harvest golden yields

No regrets
Day after day

So you and I
Say aloud
Aussie to be
We are proud

We pray
We fight
When cause
Is right

All mankind
Human rights
Australia—
Your stars are bright.
Australia—
my wonder land

While the language is simple, much of Australia's essence is contained in my father's words—courage, spirit, open spaces, and bright skies. He also expresses his devotion to the country that took him in, with phrases such as "Aussie to be—we are proud," and "Australia—my wonder land." His idealism, optimism, and hope for mankind are made clear in the last verse: he speaks of fighting for the right cause, for all mankind and for human rights, and he links this to Australia—"your stars are bright." Not a bad effort for a Polish-Jewish immigrant with hardly any formal schooling.

In the end, none of the entries submitted were considered suitable, and it was not until 1984 that a new anthem, "Advance Australia Fair," was chosen. My father's composition is more idealistic than this anthem, which is structurally more formal and uses traditional lyrics.

As well as taking a stab at the national anthem, my father composed a piece of music that he called Fantasia for Solo or Orchestra and Vocal. He was thrilled when I played this at the Fremantle Music Society. "I am very proud that it was performed publicly by my daughter," he told me. "I couldn't have asked for more in the world than to have my dear Margaret play the piece for me."

Although this book is primarily about David, it may be helpful to mention a little of what I was doing after David went to London. In the years during which David was studying at the Royal College, I was also spending a great deal of time at the piano. I had practically stopped playing during the previous four years, because I was an adolescent who wanted to assert my individuality. In addition, having David around, with his often difficult behavior, had inhibited me. Then, when David went abroad, I began practicing regularly again and took lessons with Madame Carrard. I obtained my associate in music in piano performing—an advanced music diploma issued under the auspices of the universities of Australia—which I completed in under a year, achieving good marks. In 1967, I entered the Perth finals of the Commonwealth Concerto and Vocal Competition, coming in second. In the following year I actually won the competition and was sent to Melbourne to compete in the Commonwealth final. I didn't win, but it was very exciting to have gotten so far.

A year later, at the age of twenty-three, I was back in Melbourne, where I stayed for three years, studying piano with Ada Corder, better known under her maiden name, Ada Freeman. Ada was renowned in Melbourne musical circles for having taught Nancy Weir, one of Australia's leading pianists. She was an inspiration to me; we had an excellent rapport and what was meant to be a one-hour lesson would often run to three hours at no extra cost. After the lessons, I would practice for about five hours a day on a piano that my mother's sister-in-law, Auntie Gertie, had kindly lent me. At the same time I supported myself by working part time for a law firm.

My musical life was a very full one. I appeared as a soloist with the West Australian Symphony Orchestra and the Melbourne Symphony Orchestra. The whole family came to hear me play when I appeared in Perth. My father called me "a real knock-out," and said that I had "brought the house down." I was fortunate in having very good conductors. In Perth I played under the sympathetic baton of Sir Bernard Heinze. He made me feel very special, by guiding the orchestra to take into account my own interpretation of Liszt's "Hungarian Fantasy." I gave the piece a Gypsylike flavor, and Heinze ensured that the orchestra flowed with my approach. For the Melbourne performance I played Rimsky-Korsakov's Concerto in C-sharp Minor, conducted by the distinguished Dutch conductor Willem van Otterloo. Several of my performances were broadcast on

Australian television, and I also received good write-ups in the papers.

My father always gave me a great deal of encouragement. He was not at all opposed to my leaving the family nest and becoming more independent. *Shine* wrongly portrays him as desperate to keep the family together at all costs. ("You are not going! I won't let anyone destroy this family," Peter says in the film.) The reality was quite different. For example, he wrote to me as follows:

"My dearest daughter, Here is a letter for you in reply to your last letter. I must admit that your writing looks more like music to me everyday, so keep up reading all that literature. The more the better, as my intentions are to bind all your letters and treasure them as a work of art. . . . Living away from home will make you wiser. Of course I consider now that you have reached maturity and can make up your own decisions. . . . My dearest, your ever loving pop and family XXXXXXX"

When I returned to Perth in 1971, I joined the Australian Broadcasting Commission as a secretary. In July 1973, I made my first trip abroad, traveling to England (with a few days' stopover in Singapore) and then on to Israel. I wanted to learn Hebrew, so I took a five-month course in Tel Aviv. After another year in Perth at the Australian Broadcasting Commission, I decided to move to Israel in 1975. I planned to take a degree in English Language and General History at the Hebrew University of Jerusalem. But I was in no hurry, and took a tour of sixteen European countries on the way. When I arrived in Israel, I settled in Jerusalem. Living in that beautiful city, which holds such a special place in the hearts and minds of the Jewish people, gave me great inner peace and intellectual joy.

Before I left Perth, my father and I shared a very special, silent moment, capturing the unspoken understanding we have always had. I had no idea that it was to be the last time I would see my dear father alive. There was some trepidation on my father's part that I was going to live so far away, yet he was glad it was Israel. He had been a supporter of a Jewish state throughout his life, and especially so after the Holocaust.

When I had finished my degree at the Hebrew University, I taught English and piano in two Jerusalem high schools. After a few years, I met my Scottish-born husband, Allan, a doctor who works in the main hospital in Beersheva, the capital of southern Israel's Negev desert. I settled in Beersheva and now teach piano in a small music conservatory just outside the town.

A short time after I left Australia, on December 29, 1975, my father passed away quietly and unexpectedly in his sleep, at the age of seventy-two. In many ways he died with a broken heart. It seems that along with a propensity for musical talent in our family, there is also a tendency to mental illness. It was truly a huge blow to my father to see first Hannah, his only sibling to survive the Holocaust, institutionalized and then his son David fall prey to the same affliction.

Right up to the end my father felt that while he could not cure David, he could nevertheless improve his condition with the right mixture of nutrition, exercise, deep breathing, and positive thinking. When this didn't succeed he was extremely sad. Far from being a villain, as *Shine* suggests, he had in fact devoted a large part of his life to David; so it was a terrible thing for Dad at the end to see his son in the state that he was.

Of course my father had his faults; he could be stubborn and fixed in his ideas, and Leslie found him at times domineering. But overall he was a wonderful man—principled, warm, generous, and always ready to help those in trouble.

Shine suggests that David did not attend Dad's funeral—which is not true. The film shows only a graveyard scene, which is set nine years after his death. Standing over my father's tombstone, Gillian asks David, "What do you feel?" and my brother replies, "Nothing." Gillian then asks a leading question, "Nothing at all?" to which David replies sarcastically: "Well, I'm shocked, stunned, and completely amazed—how does that sound?" Then David and Gillian walk off while, in the words of the screenplay (scene 194), "We hear joyous singing: 'Funiculi, Funicula.'" This glorious nineteenth-century Italian song by Luigi Denza is a particularly distasteful choice of music to play over my father's grave.

The reality was quite different. After Dad's death, David made it clear, both at the funeral and afterward, that he had very fond memories of his father. Certainly he never said that he felt nothing when Dad died. On the contrary, he paid tribute to our father in the newspaper two or three days later. "If I have done any good at all, I owe it to my father," David wrote.

He has also told me repeatedly in various letters how much he loved Dad. For example, on April 4, 1977, he wrote, "I'm missing Dad, I can't believe he's dead." Again, on May 23, 1978, he wrote that he was still struggling with his father's death: "It seems unreal, even though I participated at the funeral." He also told me about how impressed he was, now that he himself had studied, because it made him realize just what a broad knowledge of music my father had acquired, and how much Dad had taught him.

David praised Dad to others, too. In a letter dated January 2, 1976, to Sir Keith Falkner, director of the Royal College of Music, he wrote: "Pop was a super human being and I wish you could have met him." He added that he and the family would be in mourning for seven days, according to Jewish custom.

In fact, David never said anything negative about my father until Gillian and Scott Hicks conceived the idea of making *Shine* in 1986.

14

THE ROAD TO REHABILITATION: A GOOD WOMAN AND A FAIR MAN HELP DAVID

After my father's death, David continued to live at home with Louise, Leslie, and my mother. (Suzie, like me, had moved out.) My father's death was a huge loss to the whole family. David, in particular, took it very badly. He became terribly depressed, his health declined, and his behavior was erratic. For example, he would eat wherever he felt like it, all over the house—Leslie often discovered bits of cheese lying in unlikely places and had to plead with David not to leave food around, as it attracted mice and rats.

This period wasn't easy for the family. Those same people who had been so eager to involve themselves in David's life before and after he went to London were now no longer interested in his welfare. In May 1976, Leslie left for a long-awaited first trip abroad—to Europe, North Africa, and to visit me in Israel. Not long afterward, David's condition deteriorated fur-

ther; my mother, Suzie, and Louise held extensive discussions with David's doctor, who strongly advised
that David go back into hospital, where he could receive full-time supervision and medical care.

So David was readmitted to Graylands. Even then
his life was not without music. The hospital had a
piano for David to play on, and his favorite music re-
sounded throughout the wards. A nurse told my
mother on one of her frequent visits that David added
"tone" to the unit, and cheered everyone up with his
joyous melodies. He didn't play all the time, of
course, but he certainly wasn't barred from playing,
as has been stated numerous times in the media since
Shine's release.

After a few weeks of treatment, David's condition
improved sufficiently for him to be discharged. He
chose to go and stay for a while with Mr. and Mrs.
Price, a very good-hearted couple who lived on the
outskirts of Perth. Our family home was in a noisier
inner-city district, while the Prices lived far from
Perth's metropolis, where it would be quieter for
David and he could take long country walks.

As the fact that the father who had done so much
for him was no longer there began to sink in, David
became aware that it wasn't easy for his family to
cope with his mental illness full time. He realized that
he needed to take charge of his own life, and to his
great credit, he began to take steps toward being
more independent and responsible for himself. He
was extremely lucky at this time to meet two fantastic people, who were to help him enormously on the
road to rehabilitation.

One of them was Dorothy Croft, known to her

friends as Dot. She and David met while he was in Graylands Hospital. She was also a pianist, and was playing one evening for a choir in an outer suburb of Perth, where David, who was having a night out of the hospital, had gone to hear the choir. Someone suggested he sit next to Dot at the piano. He offered to turn the pages for her and she happily accepted, because as every pianist knows, a good page turner is invaluable. Impressed at the way he did the job, she asked the choir mistress who this man was. When she was told she was shocked. She couldn't believe it was the same David Helfgott, whose career she, like many other Perth music enthusiasts, had followed with avid interest over the years.

Dot felt a strong urge to help David and started visiting him at Graylands. She often took him to the beach for short breaks, and gradually their friendship blossomed into a close relationship. Dot told me later: "David was very romantic. He used to bring me chocolates and so on."

During the eight years in which they were seeing each other, Dot helped David enormously, encouraging him, finding him pupils for piano lessons, having him stay for weekends. She arranged concerts for him and also other activities such as tennis matches. She put his newspaper clippings in order, pasted them in scrapbooks, and labeled them according to date and category. These are the clippings that my father is shown burning in *Shine*.

My mother liked Dot tremendously. She often wrote to me about the outings on which she accompanied David and Dot. When I was on a trip back home, I went with her and David to visit Dot. I could immediately sense what a warm atmosphere there was in Dot's home, and what a genuinely kind person she is. David and I had a lovely time playing duets on Dot's two pianos. It was great fun, and felt just like old times. David seemed to be in the best of health, and very happy with Dot.

In 1977, David decided to look around for a suitable place to live and this is when the second person who was to prove such a help to him appeared. The Reverend Robert Fairman was a Methodist minister who ran a halfway house (Bassendean Lodge) licensed by the Australian government for people with emotional and psychiatric problems. David sought his help and instantly liked the lodge. For the next seven years he was cared for by this remarkable man, first in Bassendean and afterward in another district of Perth, where the lodge was reestablished under the name Gildercliffe Lodge.

I have spoken to the Reverend Fairman and he told me that when David came to inspect the lodge, the first thing he did was to take a look at the bedroom and the second was to ask if they had a piano. They did, and after playing it he remarked that it was better than the piano he had been playing at the Selby Centre, a local government-run mental-health rehabilitation organization where he was then working as a book binder.

"When David came to me I knew nothing about his background," said the Reverend Fairman. "I saw a young man, rather scholarly in appearance, quite intelligent in speech and conversation, displaying a nervous little laugh and overly polite. David played the piano from the day he arrived. In fact, he made it his own. At Bassendean we moved the piano to an un-used building a little way away from the main build-ing, where David could play undisturbed. However, he loved an audience, and would often shout to the residents at the top of his voice, asking whether they had a 'favorite.' David did not confine himself to the classics. Since I am Irish-born I would often request 'Danny Boy' or 'The Rose of Tralee.' The theme from the movie *The Sting* was particularly popular with some of the other residents."

My mother, Leslie, Suzie, and Louise went to see David regularly. Leslie tried to help David in many ways—not only as an emotionally supportive brother, but also more practically. He gave David all sorts of small gifts that he felt would make his life more com-fortable. He bought him a television set and gave him money whenever he needed it.

I went to see David at the lodge during a return visit from Israel in 1980. The place was very pleasant, with billiards, table tennis, darts, and so on, and a staff of fourteen to look after residents' needs. David went out a lot and soon knew the area well. He often went swimming in the clear waters of the nearby Indian Ocean. He was very popular with his fellow residents, both men and women, who included some of the kindest and most gentle people imaginable. At Bassendean, David tutored a couple of students and enjoyed a busy social life. This continued after the lodge moved.

"When we moved to Gildercliffe Lodge, we pulled the extra bed out of David's room and placed David's piano in his bedroom for his own exclusive use," the Reverend Fairman told me, adding, "David gave lots of concerts. There was many an evening when my sister-in-law helped David fix his bow tie and brush down his tuxedo. As well as giving concerts, David also taught advanced-grade pupils in this period. He probably had the most active social life of any of the fifty residents at the lodge. He went out late most evenings and away at weekends. In fact, he was the only resident to be given his own key to the front door. David lived a full social life—a monk he was not! Very often some lady would appear at the front door to take David to a function or whatever. In particular, he met Dot Croft. Everyone knew about this because the residents' phone was located right at the center of the lodge, and everyone could hear—in most cases to their great amusement—David's loud affirmations of affection."

Contrary to what has been stated in hundreds of media reports all around the world about *Shine,* David gave many public performances during his stay at the lodge. In 1978 he appeared as a special guest artist at a concert to raise money for his old high school, the John Forrest Senior High School. He played piano duets with a local musician, Helen Dear, including one of his favorites, "Spanish Dance No. 2," by Moszkowski, a nineteenth-century Polish-German pianist and composer.

David also appeared many times in public together with Leslie, who was now working as a violin teacher and a musician. These were very popular affairs. My brothers had been making a name for themselves and the concerts were usually sold out and attracted press interest. For example, they gave a series of concerts at the Subiaco Theatre Centre about which *Music*

Maker magazine ran a two-page article headlined "Ladies and Gentlemen . . . It's the Helfgott Brothers."

David also began playing with the Karrinyup Symphony Orchestra, for which Leslie already played second violin. Dot took David to rehearsals with the orchestra and for concert appearances. The conductor was none other than Frank Arndt, our first piano teacher, who once again spent much time encouraging David, as he had done in the past. On one particularly memorable evening on November 9, 1980, David played the Bach D Minor Concerto with the orchestra. It must have been a nostalgic occasion for him, because he had first played it when he was only twelve years old. Even then he received excellent reviews, much better ones than he gets now. "Helfgott's lyrical style was a pleasure to hear," wrote music critic Barbara Yates Rothwell. Under the headline "Tunes of Glory," Derek Moore Morgan, the music critic of *The West Australian,* wrote: "David Helfgott negotiated the considerable pianistic pitfalls of Balakirev's 'Islamey' with fluency and clarity."

David's rehabilitation took a further step forward when Leslie found him a job playing the piano three nights a week at Riccardo's Restaurant and Wine Bar in September 1983. Riccardo's is the bar shown in the opening scene in *Shine,* where it is renamed "Moby's."

I was already in Israel at this time, but family and friends kept me informed of David's popularity and success at Riccardo's. They sent me videos of David playing, surrounded by an appreciative and enthusiastic audience. His adoring fans plied him with cigarettes and drinks, entranced by his music. He had enormous fun, as did the customers, when he played Rimsky-Korsakov's "Flight of the Bumble Bee" or one of his other favorites. My family often went to see him play and it warmed their hearts to see him so happy, and to hear the cheering of the audience. Even Madame Carrard turned up. "I don't usually go to this kind of bar at my age," she told me later, "but I had a marvelous time."

David received a lot of local press publicity, and was attracting large crowds who came to hear him play. He would often joke with the customers. When patrons asked David to play Beethoven's Fifth, David would reply with a grin: "Which one? Symphony or Concerto?" (Beethoven wrote nine symphonies, and five piano concertos. One of David's special talents was that he could also play symphonies that had been transcribed for the piano.) He was described in the press as "leering mischievously through bottle-lensed spectacles." David's appearances at Riccardo's became such an event that when he finally stopped playing there in 1986, *Music Maker* magazine ran a cover story entitled "Riccardo's—The Party's Over."

These were not the only concerts David was giving. In July 1984, he played Rachmaninoff's Second Piano Concerto with the Nedlands Symphony Orchestra at Winthrop Hall at the University of Western Australia under the baton of the Polish conductor Henryk Pisarek. ("Winthrop Hall has seldom seen such a huge crowd. David Helfgott gave it all the lyricism, sensitivity, and passion we had come to hear and the audience responded with great warmth," wrote critic Jan Shepherd in *Music Maker*.) David also played with his beloved teacher, Madame Carrard, on

May 25, 1985, at a special concert at the Octagon Theatre, which is situated on the campus of the University of Western Australia. They played both solo and two-piano works to great acclaim, including Milhaud's "Scaramouche." On November 16, 1985, David and Katie Hewgill played the Rachmaninoff Sonata for Cello and Piano, at the same venue. In 1986, David gave three more concerts at the Octagon Theatre, selling out over 2,000 seats at this octagonal-shaped venue. His program included three preludes by Rachmaninoff and one of his favorites, "Pictures at an Exhibition," by Mussorgsky. All the concerts were very well received. One was even broadcast on television.

It was during the period in which he was playing at Riccardo's that David met Gillian Murray, a divorcee and a professional astrologer with two grown children. From then on David's relationship with Dot abruptly ended and she found herself dramatically shut out of his life. Gillian had been introduced to David by the owner of Riccardo's, Dr. Chris Reynolds, and several months later, on August 26, 1984, they married. My family in Perth attended the wedding. (Gillian and Reynolds fell out badly over the making of *Shine,* so the character in the film who is directly based on Reynolds was changed to an attractive blond woman.)

After they were married, David and Gillian began to make trips abroad. I met them in London in 1986 at Rudolph Steiner House, and David and I had great fun playing Dvorak's New World Symphony, a wonderful piece arranged as a piano duet, which we used to love performing together as children.

David and his new wife traveled all over Europe in the late 1980s. He gave many concerts, performing in, among other locations, Vienna, Sion (in Switzerland), Budapest, Helsinki, Oslo, Copenhagen, Bonn, and Düsseldorf. In 1988 they came to visit me in Israel. David gave a private recital in Jerusalem at the house of a friend of mine. My husband and I took Gillian and David touring. He particularly loved visiting the ancient Jewish mountain fortress of Masada, and the Dead Sea, which is the lowest point on earth, and we all had a great time.

David also went to London, where he studied with Peter Feuchtwanger, a German music professor from Munich who had lived in London since the 1970s. Later, in October 1994, David returned to give a concert at the Royal College of Music. I was very pleased for him and his successes.

David has undoubtedly spent some exciting years with Gillian. She has taught him several new skills, such as yoga, and she has tried hard to bring his nicotine and caffeine addictions under control. (At one stage David was smoking over 130 cigarettes a day and drinking about twenty-five cups of coffee.) In many respects, Gillian has made David very happy and for this the whole Helfgott family is grateful to her. But in other ways, David has changed for the worse. When Gillian met David, he was well on the way to recovery. He had had the benefit of seven caring years with Reverend Fairman and almost eight with Dorothy Croft. He was reasonably independent, playing with his brother Leslie, and performing with various orchestras. He could, for example, catch public transport by himself without difficulties. He had his own bank account. Yet when I saw him in 1988 in Israel, he was already manifesting some rather peculiar habits. For example, when catching sight of our dog, David exclaimed: "Is it a cat? Is it a wolf?" and finally, "Is it a dog?"

Later, in 1991, when I saw David in Perth, he spoke in an even more unusual way: He said to me over and over again: "Hello Margaret, hello Margaret, hello Margaret, hello Margaret, my Santa Margarita." I was quite mystified, as David had never talked like that before. And as time went by he became more and more hyperactive, talking rapidly and leaping from one subject to another.

Another equally serious development was afoot. After marrying Gillian, David started saying things (and more specifically telling journalists things) that are completely untrue. I don't believe that David says these statements of his own volition. I believe Gillian, who has herself said some pretty nasty things, encourages him to talk in this way. Certainly the habit became more marked after Gillian got together with Scott Hicks in 1986 and they began to plan *Shine.* The derogatory remarks about people who had helped David in the past coincided with the appearance of articles praising Gillian for "rescuing" David. Thus began Gillian's myth building.

I was particularly concerned because it was not just my family, but other good people who were being trampled on by Gillian to promote herself and what she considered was best for David. I met the Reverend Bob Fairman again for a long talk in 1996, after *Shine* had come out. This kind Christian man, with his ready smile and engaging, gentle manner, poured his heart out to me. He had looked after David for seven years; now he was on the verge of tears as he outlined the cruel things Gillian Helfgott and Scott Hicks (and sometimes also David) had been saying about the period when David was with him. Numerous articles and television and radio programs around the world talked about David "lying and dying on floors of halfway houses," being denied access to the piano, and so on.

"David was not 'locked up in mental hospitals.' This is all a myth," said the Reverend Fairman. "When he was at the lodge, which was most of the time, he was free to come and go, visit his family, give concerts, have girlfriends, go on holidays—and he did all of these things. At the same time, he received proper medical supervision in a caring and professional environment, which is, of course, what people who have these kinds of mental problems need."

The Reverend Fairman was distraught about the things that David has said about the lodge since he met Gillian. "Some of the remarks are just absurd— that we didn't have any knives and forks, for instance. Can you imagine fifty people eating three cooked meals every day without cutlery? David did not bury his face in a lady's crotch, as has been claimed, nor even touch one in an unseemly way. Nor did he run around naked. During the time he was with us, he was much more coherent than he is now. In spite of his nervous disposition, he radiated a quiet dignity and was most gentlemanly. Contrary to the numerous newspaper reports, he was a free agent. I had no authority to tell David what to do, nor did I ever try. He had a very enjoyable time at the lodge. It was a pressure-free environment and he had plenty of friends."

My brother's calm state is confirmed in official reports by his doctors. For example, a report prepared by a consultant physician in March 1983, just before David met Gillian, states that my brother's "speech was normal throughout the interview." It can also be seen on interviews he gave to Australian TV discussing concerts he was giving during this period, programs such as the ABC's *Nationwide* (January 1984), and Nine Network's *Mike Willesee Show* (July 1984), broadcast a month before he married Gillian. It would not have been difficult for Scott Hicks to obtain videos of these programs.

David was not "released from dark years in an institution" as one paper put it following an interview with Gillian, describing life at the lodge as "a nightmare." The lodge had a reputation for excellence; the Reverend Fairman has even received parliamentary citations for his work. In March 1984, Barry Hodge, Western Australia's Minister for Health, wrote a special letter, "commending the Reverend Fairman for his valuable work on behalf of the state of Western Australia." And in April 1986, Graham Burkett, a member of Western Australia's Legislative Assembly wrote: "The Reverend Fairman is one of the most respected and highly regarded persons in Western Australia and his hostel is often displayed by the government as an example to persons operating similar hostels."

Fairman is not the kind of man to run to his lawyers. Yet in 1987 he became the first of several people involved in this sorry saga to contemplate legal action against Gillian Helfgott. In July of that year he instructed his lawyer to send a letter threatening a defamation suit against her for remarks she had made in *The Australian Women's Weekly*. She had said that David "lived in a room like a cell," was "sedated into almost catatonic state" and had been "left to suffer alone." The Reverend Fairman warned her not to repeat these allegations.

Gillian also claimed that David "hadn't played [the music which he then played at Riccardo's] for almost fifteen years," which is simply not true. I myself heard him play when I visited the lodge in 1980. Other residents and staff at the lodge also protested that this article was "misleading and totally inaccurate."

The Reverend Fairman told me that after this episode, when he heard that Gillian and Scott Hicks were planning to make a film, he had telephoned the film company in Adelaide; but no one had got back to him and he was never interviewed for *Shine* or shown a copy of the script. Sometime later, when he heard further rumors of all the untrue things that were to be included, he rang again and eventually managed to speak to the screenwriter. The Reverend Fairman said he was assured that he had no need for concern—the film was to be highly dramatized and, he gathered, fictitious. "I was very surprised," the Reverend Fairman said to me, "when I saw that *Shine* was being described as a true story. I was shocked to see the character supposedly representing myself locking the piano away from David—I never did anything like that. The filmmakers' line of thinking must have been: Why let facts spoil a good story?

"David was in a far better shape when he was

under my care than he is now. He is an intelligent man, and you could then hold an intelligent conversation with him. He often went home to see his family and they often came to visit. In the whole seven years, David never said one angry word against his father."

The Reverend Fairman also described how in 1984 he went with his wife to David and Gillian's wedding. "At the wedding reception I heard Gillian say to David 'It's toilet time, David. Come along to the toilet.' David never had to be told this when he lived at the lodge. He never groped women as he does in *Shine*. He did not babble as he does now. He talked normally. In fact, he was charming and a gentleman.

"I admire and love David Helfgott very deeply," he added, "and it is greatly distressing to see the words now coming out of his mouth. I think if he realized the hurt that these untrue things he is saying to journalists are causing, he would be deeply hurt himself."

By 1997, the Reverend Fairman had had enough. He fired off several angry letters to newspaper editors. The one to the *Los Angeles Times* read as follows:

"Dear Sir,

My attention has been drawn to an article in your newspaper (March 24, 1997) by Mr. Scott Hicks. In seeking to defend himself, sadly he forces me to defend myself and my work among the emotionally disturbed. In saying that Mr. David Helfgott 'lay on the floor,' 'abandoned,' 'out of sight' of those who now 'profess' such concern for him, Mr. Hicks betrays a mean strategy, namely throwing muck in a different direction.

These unkind accusations were compounded by Mr. Hicks in a television interview in which he added 'sick and dying.' Nothing could be further from the truth. David came to my home, discharged from hospital and almost immediately enjoyed a fairly active social life. In my home he taught piano, as he did also in the home of Mrs. Dot Croft. Daily he caught a train to work as a book binding employee. Most evenings he was out attending functions, or actually performing at some concert . . ."

It is not only the Reverend Fairman who is distressed at the falsities Gillian has been feeding the media. Writing to the editor-in-chief of *The Australian Women's Weekly* on June 26, 1987, Dorothy Croft said:

"I wish to protest in the strongest possible terms about your scurrilous and inaccurate article. The content is sickening to those who know the truth about this pianist's life . . . I can't believe that a reputable magazine could lower its standards by printing such things . . . David was not 'locked up in a cell, deserted and alone.' He had security, care, and love."

Dot's letter goes on to outline in great detail David's concerts, friends, and social and sporting activities. "David's life did not begin again when he walked into Riccardo's restaurant in 1983. This myth has been promulgated in a large number of articles that have been written about David Helfgott and it is high time that it was shattered into a million little pieces." The publisher of *The Australian Women's Weekly,* Richard Walsh, confirmed in reply to Dot's letter that information for the article had been supplied by Gillian and David.

Later Dot told me: "In all the years that I knew David, he never once said anything derogatory about his father. I was amazed when I read newspaper interviews in which he said things like 'Daddy was cruel.' I wondered why in the world he was saying these things, and I can't believe that they can be his own thoughts."

It's clear that the myth-making originates (to a large extent at least) from Gillian, while at the same time she promotes herself as David's rescuer. For example, describing the period between his return from London in 1970 and his first meeting with her in 1983, Gillian is quoted in *The Herald* newspaper on May 30, 1986, as saying: "Imagine him locked up in an institution for twelve years. Sometimes they wouldn't even let him play the piano. He suffered from severe loneliness with no one to ever care about him."

In *Shine,* David is referred to as "a stray dog," as he wanders into "Moby's" by himself in 1983. Had Scott Hicks done his research (or spoken to me or Leslie or others), he would have come across positive reviews of David's music such as the ones already referred to dated November 10, 1980. Now, as a result of the film, endless newspaper articles have stated with apparent authority that David didn't perform in public between his return from London and 1983, when he came "under the watchful eye of his wife Gillian." The magazine *New Idea* carried an article along these lines on August 24, 1985, under the title "The Love That Reclaimed a Lost Genius."

I have found that once journalists become familiar with Gillian's and *Shine*'s version, it is very difficult to persuade them to publish the truth. The myths become the facts. Before his marriage to Gillian, it was a different story. For example, *The West Australian* (December 17, 1983) praised "His girlfriend Dorothy Croft." *The National Times* (January 6, 1984) stated that "the dramatic turnaround in Helfgott has been wrought by his girlfriend Dorothy Croft . . . and his manager Chris Reynolds."

The many long letters David wrote to me in Israel from 1975 to 1983, most of which I have kept (but to which Gillian holds the copyright), also tell a different tale. They are without exception upbeat and positive, with dozens of references to attending or playing in concerts, to lessons with Madame Carrard, and to auditions at the ABC and elsewhere. David mentions his concerts with Leslie, playing cards with Leslie, and going out dancing with Mom. He writes with enthusiasm of his leisure activities, of the tennis he played and the Chinese restaurant he ate in. He also refers sympathetically to his first wife Claire, and to the "happy days" of his childhood. He praises life at the hostel. His letter of April 4, 1977, tells about the "good friends" he had made. On May 23, 1978, he wrote: "The hostel is very nice and I have good friends there."

Leslie, who visited David throughout this period, confirms all this: "During the time he spent at the

Reverend Fairman's lodges, David was very happy. He had good food, a good bed, and a piano. He had his independence. The lodge was the best place for David to be at that time. It was very positive for his mental health. It was really excellent therapy and his condition improved no end."

This is the accurate version of events before Gillian entered David's life. The distortion of the truth as presented in *Shine* has done nothing but hurt a great many decent people. The only person who has benefited is Gillian.

15

THE MAKING OF *SHINE*

—————

While I was on a visit to Perth in June 1986, my sister Suzie was contacted by a film director who was in town. He said he was going to make a movie about David and the Helfgott family, and wanted to talk to us about it. When Suzie told me about this, my initial reaction was to be cautious. I had no idea who Scott Hicks was, and I thought that a stranger wanting to put our family in full view of the world might well result in an invasion of privacy. We were not, after all, public figures and had not sought a life in the public eye.

Hicks said he had already spoken with Gillian and David, but they had not mentioned anything to us. I thought it would have been more appropriate to ask us first. I was also a little wary because of the articles that had been appearing in the press since David met Gillian, which had distorted David's past. At the time

I attributed these distortions to media exaggeration, rather than to any kind of deliberate attempt to build myths around David. Still, Suzie and I decided that if a film was going to be made, it would be better to co-operate and ensure that it was accurate.

Hicks said he had come up with the idea for the film after reading a newspaper report about David and then attending one of his concerts. He interviewed Suzie and myself in his hotel. I told him about Dad's life in Poland, the family background, our childhood, and so on. I asked him what sort of movie he had in mind and whether it was meant to be a real life story or a work of fiction, but he didn't give me a clear answer.

We heard no more and after some time I assumed the project must have been dropped. Then, more than two years later, in August 1988, Leslie, Suzie, and Louise contacted me in Israel. They were very distressed. They said that some advance publicity for the film had appeared out of the blue, and that it contained some very disturbing phrases in connection with my father, such as "from patience to tyranny"; it also said that our family had "shunned" David on his return from London. I wrote to Hicks straightaway, telling him that I was concerned about these statements. I told him that my father had been "a man of talent, strength and conviction, with a capacity for great love" and that he "absolutely adored David." I asked him not to "detract from the truth," and I said that I was worried that there might be negative repercussions for David's fragile state of health should his life story be handled in the wrong way. In addition I asked him if he could kindly show me a copy of the script. Leslie also expressed his objections to Hicks.

I had heard that Gillian was involved in the film project and so on the same day I wrote to Hicks, I also wrote to her. I told her how worried I was by the film's promotional material. "I would feel so much more secure," I wrote, "if I could know that you would not let anything appear in the film that might harm David, the other Helfgotts, or my father's memory, something that would be regretted later, and which may cause irrevocable damage to David."

It was not until the following year—more than four months later—that Hicks replied to my letter. On January 6, 1989, he wrote to dispel my fears. He said: "It is not my intention to be judgmental in the portrayal of Peter Helfgott . . . I would ask you not to attach excessive importance to the wording you quote from the brochure as this is a very brief summary intended only to attract interest in the idea, and conveys none of the balance of the approach." He reassured me by saying that the more communication there was among all of us, the greater the chance that the "true" story would be told. But despite his apparent desire for closer ties, this was the only letter I ever received from him. Rereading it today, I realize that his interest then had not been in "balancing the approach," or in increased communication; he had wanted to soothe me and keep me quiet, rather than to seriously consider my objections.

A few days later Gillian phoned to inform me that a journalist, Kirsty Cockburn, would be writing a book about David and our family. When Kirsty called me the following week and told me she had been

commissioned by Gillian, she was genuinely surprised when I told her I had only just heard about it.
She thought I had been involved in the project from
the beginning. In retrospect, I realize the plans for a
book and a film were linked. It seems that in both
cases the idea was to tell David's life story from
Gillian's point of view, to promote his career, and to
portray herself as his savior.

I wrote to Gillian on January 22, 1989, saying that
I did not think signing contracts for films and books
without first talking them over with the rest of the
family, was the best way of going about things. At the
time there were rumors in the family that Gillian and
David would get a 5 percent share of the profits of
the film and apparently this had then been reduced
to 2½ percent, which had upset Gillian. Gillian wrote
back to me on February 18, 1989, denying that contracts had been signed. (I have no evidence whether
they actually had or not.)

A great deal of correspondence then took place between myself and the family, and also between
Gillian and myself. Leslie said he was not opposed to
a book or a film as long as it was a truthful account,
and did not contain the kind of lies that had been
written about my father in the advance publicity.
Leslie, Suzie, and I made legal inquiries, and discovered that one cannot defame the dead, only the living. This came as a shock to me. It meant that anyone
could make a film or write a book about someone
precious to you and say whatever they liked, and you
could do nothing about it.

Some years passed and, to my great relief, I was
told that the film was on hold because Hicks had

failed to raise sufficient finance. Then in December 1994, I received a letter from Gillian and David letting me know that the film would be going ahead. (At that stage Gillian and I were still maintaining a regular and fairly amiable correspondence. In effect all David's letters since 1984 had been written by Gillian—he no longer wrote me letters of his own.)

Gillian told me that the film would be made with the backing of Pandora Films in Paris, the BBC in England, and the FFC in Australia, and that actors had been cast. She wrote that the film's main theme, apart from the music, would be David's relationship with my father. She also told me that at the end of the film there would be "a most moving and beautiful resolution of the relationship with Peter." She went on to say that David "feels very deeply that your father would be pleased about the film and he also feels a great peace with Peter." She mentioned that Leslie, Suzie, and Louise had raised some questions about the film and expressed a wish to see the script. She had read the first version of the script and she told me that it would not in her opinion "cause pain to anyone portrayed in it." She added that Scott Hicks would be flying to Perth to "personally share with the family his concepts and also discuss any matters the family want to share with him."

At the time, Gillian's words reassured me a great deal—perhaps, after all, the film would turn out be a tribute to Dad's enormous role in David's development as a pianist. Filming was to begin in April 1995. I wrote back to Gillian asking whether the film would use our real names. I also again told her of the family's concerns and said I would like to see the script for myself, especially since I had heard that I would be portrayed in the film. I said that "once the film will have the wholehearted blessing of the Helfgott family, it can only be a source of pride for all of us, and for all who have the honor to know David and appreciate his genius." Gillian never replied to my question about whether real or fictional names would be used.

In February 1995, Scott Hicks brought the script to Perth. His intention was to allow some of the family to see it, but only under very restricted circumstances. My mother wasn't given access to the script. I was told by my family that Hicks refused to send me the script because of its "confidentiality." He also insisted on being present during the entire time Leslie, Suzie, and Louise read it.

"I couldn't possibly read and absorb an 111-page script in the time I was given, and I am sure Hicks knew this," Leslie told me. "Hicks said he could come round to my house at 7:00 a.m. He said we would have two hours to read the script as he had to be somewhere else at 9:30, and we couldn't hold on to a copy. With my young children running around, it was impossible for me properly to take the script in. Although I did not have time to finish reading the whole script, I did manage to make several objections, for example over the burning of press clippings. Hicks said it was 'symbolic.' I replied 'nothing like this ever happened, Scott. It's not the kind of thing my father would have done.' Then Hicks said he had to go."

Louise, too, objected to some scenes. Suzie said

she found the fact that we were called by our real names "rather scary."

I now realize that the claim that the script was too confidential for the family to read properly—or, in the case of my mother and me, to see at all—was patently untrue. I have discovered that nonfamily members were allowed to keep copies of the script for many days. For example, Rabbi Ronnie Figdor of Adelaide, the advisor on Jewish content for the film, says he was given a copy to retain on February 3.

I phoned Hicks several times asking to see a copy of the script, leaving messages on his answering machine. I asked him to please call me back. He didn't. On May 13, 1995, when filming was already well under way, I sent him a telegram in which I said I would be "grateful to hear what arrangements there were for me to see the script. With thanks." Again he did not reply. Now that I know that the screenplay attributes to my character such repulsive lines as "This house is like a concentration camp" (scene 54), I realize why he was doing everything he could to avoid me.

Gillian then called me on May 17, 1995, telling me that there were "problems" with regard to the book Kirsty Cockburn was writing and that she had in due course asked another writer, Beverley Eley, instead. Eley, whose first biography of the Australian writer Ion Idriess was widely praised, was later also to fall out with Gillian. In marked contrast to Hicks's approach, during the course of her writing she looked into the information she had been supplied by Gillian and David, and found that in many cases she had been misled. But although she managed to make a number of last-minute changes to her book, in many instances it was too late. She had been given a very short time to write *The Book of David,* published by HarperCollins, and as it was hitting the bookstores, she realized that many parts of it were still inaccurate and misleading.

Since then, others—such as the Reverend Fairman—have been in touch with her to put right more aspects of her account. Beverley Eley has in fact decided to undertake the not inconsiderable task of rewriting the whole book. Eley told *Who Weekly* (December 9, 1996) that: "I could find no evidence that this man (Peter Helfgott) deserves any of this portrayal at all (in *Shine*). More than a third of the film is spent building up this picture of Peter Helfgott as a monster. It's not the way it was." She has also had the decency to apologize to me and others.

Nevertheless, Eley had managed to correct a number of errors before publication, and as a result there were wide discrepancies between *The Book of David*—which was published at the same time as *Shine* was released — and the film's version of David's life. Gillian was furious. Eley claims that Gillian contacted bookshops and journalists to try to persuade them that her book should not be sold. Gillian even told one Melbourne newspaper that Eley was "bitchy." Eley is now considering whether to instigate court proceedings against Gillian. "I have endured emotional suffering and distress by Gillian Helfgott falsely and erroneously telling others that my biography was inaccurate, unprofessional and deficient," an extremely angry Eley told me.

On June 19, 1995, I again wrote to Scott Hicks

pointing out that I hadn't received a reply to my telegram, and that I had just learned from Louise that there was a scene in the script in which my father hits my mother (scene 48). I reiterated: "My father was not a violent man." Hicks never replied to this letter, either. (In any event, this scene was removed from the film, following Louise's strenuous objections, but it remains in the official screenplay published some months after *Shine*'s release.)

There were more shocks to come. A friend sent me an article, entitled "On Location," from the June 26, 1995, edition of *Encore* magazine. I shuddered when I read that *Shine*'s director of photography, Geoffrey Simpson, had said that there were scenes in the film when "David's father beat him." Then, in January 1996, the young actress who plays me in the film, Rebecca Gooden, wrote me a lovely letter, which I was very touched by. She said she was excited to be in a major film, and that she wanted to be in touch with the "real Margaret." But she also sent me an interview with herself from the latest issue of *Disney Adventures*. In it she says (in all innocence), "Margaret is ignored by her father . . . There is a lot of anger, jealousy, and violence in the film." I was stunned and upset by these statements. Hicks had not even had the decency to reply to my letters and phone calls, yet he and the screenwriter felt it was perfectly fine to reinvent my childhood.

After the film was completed, Hicks was eager to ensure there would be no hitches with regard to securing favorable publicity. His attitude to the Helfgott family seems to have been one of damage limitation. In May 1996 he said he wanted to come to Perth and show the finished product to the family and then take them out to dinner. My mother was so distraught after she saw the film that she cried and refused to go to the restaurant. However, Leslie decided to go along, partly out of courtesy and partly in the hope that he could persuade Hicks to insert a disclaimer stating that *Shine* was a work of fiction.

Leslie told me later: "Part of my initial reaction was that it was artistically a very good piece of cinema and Geoffrey Rush had done a pretty good job playing David with all his quirky behavior. But I also felt very uneasy at the way Dad was portrayed. I told Hicks some of the things that were wrong in the hope that he would insert a prominent disclaimer, but he brushed my objections aside. He seemed eager to keep me quiet. He said: 'You know, there will be so much publicity around the film. I am sure you don't want to be bothered by the press. We could arrange to install unlisted numbers for you and your mother if you like, so you won't be bothered.' I, of course, refused."

Naturally, I wanted to see the film, so I contacted the distribution company, Ronin Films, and told them that I was going to be in London and asked to see it. The woman in charge of public relations was very cooperative and arranged a private screening for me in London on June 26. After seeing it I felt numb; it was surreal. Here were people called Peter, David, and Margaret Helfgott. But this was not me or my family or anyone I recognized. Of course I was happy that some of David's genius had been acknowledged, but I also wondered what my father had done to deserve being turned into this evil brute.

Hicks's approach hadn't been in the slightest bit balanced and there was no "beautiful resolution between Dad and David at the end of the film" as Gillian had promised in her letter. The last we "see" of my father is in the highly unpleasant graveyard scene. As the film ended, I searched for some sort of disclaimer that would inform the audience and the critics that the film was essentially a work of fiction, but I could find none.

To my surprise, Scott Hicks, who was in London himself, had heard that I was in town and had turned up at the private screening. It seems that he was concerned that I, like Leslie, was somewhat of a loose cannon, and he wanted to keep me from causing any trouble. Here was the opportunity to speak to him for the first time in ten years. I had been so stunned by the film that I couldn't express myself properly. I told him again that my father was nothing like the way he was portrayed, but he avoided answering me directly. When I asked him about the disclaimer, he assured me fervently that there was one but that I hadn't noticed it.

I now know why I hadn't noticed it. It must be one of the hardest-to-spot disclaimers in the history of cinema. It appears several minutes after the film has ended, stays on the screen for a very short time, and is in type so small as to be barely legible. (At a showing a friend of mine went to in a Tel Aviv movie theater, the projector was shut off as the disclaimer appeared.) On the other hand, 279 names of cast and crew members appear in much larger type at the end of the film and stay on screen for much longer. For example, the credit for "gaffer" stays on the screen for ten seconds.

In even larger type at the beginning of the credits are the words: "With thanks to David and Gillian Helfgott for their assistance and cooperation in the making of this film." This, combined with the marketing-hype and the absence of a proper disclaimer, ensured that virtually everyone believed that what they were seeing was essentially a true story. I doubt whether more than a tiny handful of the millions who have seen *Shine* stayed throughout the entire list of credits and were then actually able to read the disclaimer. I only managed finally to do so by using the pause button on my video. The disclaimer reads: "While the characters David and Gillian Helfgott are actual persons, this film also depicts characters and events which are fictional, which do not and are not intended to refer to any real person or any actual event."

Had this disclaimer been properly displayed, I doubt that newspapers would have dared to suggest Peter Helfgott was "gestapolike" (*Tri-City Herald,* Pasco, Washington) or a "monster inside with fangs and blood intact" (*Los Angeles Times*).

Later, when the screenplay was published, I was not surprised to see that the disclaimer had been removed altogether—of course, had it appeared on paper people would have had a far better chance of reading it. The screenplay does however find space to devote two pages to the cast list at the beginning and a further nine pages at the end to the crew list and music credits. Everyone from the "carpenter" to the "bar mitzvah advisor" is listed, but there seems to be no room to mention that the film is not true.

The premiere of *Shine* took place in Adelaide, Australia, on August 2, 1996. I decided not to attend, even though I was to be in Australia that month. My mother also refused to go. Leslie went as he wanted to gauge the audience reaction. By now he was exasperated. He had pleaded in vain with the producer, the film company, the public relations people, and anyone else he could find, to convey the truth about my father in the interviews and hype that was building up around *Shine,* but to no avail. He said he now felt like standing outside the official opening and holding up a huge banner saying, "My father was not a cruel person as shown in this film." (In any event, he did not do this.)

Since I realized that from an artistic point of view, *Shine* was a film of high quality, and would no doubt be greeted with critical acclaim, it began to dawn on me that there would be a mass of newspaper articles about my family. Yet it still came as a shock when I started reading them. One of the first papers to comment on *Shine* was *The Herald,* and this set the tone for 99 percent of the articles that were to follow, first in Australia and then in almost every corner of the globe. It said: "Helfgott suffered a complete breakdown . . . partly as a result of his . . . pathologically domineering father."

Moreover, the preview scene most commonly being used on television was one where my father beats up my brother. As I flicked from channel to channel, this scene seemed to pop up practically everywhere I turned. It was simply bizarre. I wanted to pinch myself, hoping that I would wake up from this nightmare. I just couldn't believe it was happening.

Leslie and I soon started getting phone calls from journalists, asking about "the beatings" that my father administered. Naturally we told them the truth. After that people we knew, but some of whom we hadn't heard from for years, rang us up, expressing distress at the film's inaccuracies. There was the Reverend Bob Fairman from Gildercliffe Lodge, our music teachers, Frank Arndt and Madame Carrard, David's first wife, Claire, his close friend of eight years, Dot, and a host of former friends and work colleagues of my father's. One by one, I began to realize that a film had been made about my brother and yet almost none of the people who had been closely involved with him had been interviewed or consulted—even though in some cases they had, like myself, specifically made themselves available. Some felt the need to speak out publicly against the film. Frank Arndt, for example, told an Australian newspaper that my father was "a very gentle and intelligent man. I got to know Peter well. He never came across as harsh."

The Perth premiere of *Shine* took place on Thursday, August 15. That night I received a phone call from Scott Hicks, who was in town for the event. He invited me for breakfast the next morning, saying he wanted to "catch up" with me before he left for Adelaide. I was rather surprised, but decided to accept his invitation, hoping that perhaps there was still a way of salvaging my father's reputation. Would he perhaps go on the record and tell the media that his portrayal in *Shine* was fictional? Hicks informed me that Gillian would pick me up in her car and bring me to the Sheraton hotel where he was staying.

But when I heard what Hicks had to say, I could hardly swallow my scrambled eggs. I was admonished for speaking out against the film, I was told I was "harming" it, and that if I continued to speak out, the media would get involved and my family would be harassed by reporters and have no peace. I was further informed that this wasn't fair on my family because I was going back to Israel and they would have to handle all the press barrage and so forth. I replied that the way my father had been depicted made it absolutely necessary for me to speak out on his behalf. I again asked for a prominent disclaimer; this time Hicks refused point-blank. He said I was "devious, manipulative, and jealous." He spoke to me in a threatening tone, hinting that he could cause trouble for me. At one point Gillian dissolved in tears. Hicks, who had apparently been left with the impression after our London meeting that he had managed to persuade me to stay quiet, was now angry with me for my comments to journalists. He said he wouldn't leave until I promised I would no longer speak to the press. I left the meeting feeling extremely scared. I was petrified at the idea of my family being harassed, so I agreed not to make any more public comments.

Late the next night I received an abusive phone call from Gillian. She said: "I'm sick of the way you're going on. You're crapping all over everything." She also patronized me, calling me "my lass," and was extremely aggressive and nasty, asking me: "Do you want your mom to be harassed?"

Although, from a mixture of fear and concern for

my mother, I had agreed to hold my tongue, a few weeks later—as the media blitz intensified—I could take it no more. Article after article appeared describing my father in the most dreadful terms. The final straw came when I picked up a copy of what is probably the world's leading news magazine, *Time* (September 23, 1996), and read that David was "prodded into prodigy status and tormented toward a nervous breakdown." I realized that my conscience would not allow me any longer to sit back and fail to stand up for the truth, for my father and also indirectly for "the true" David. Leslie and I, the two eldest children, began to speak up openly about the injustice that had been done. We wrote to newspapers. Leslie agreed to be interviewed on radio and television. He went to a film projectionist to obtain the exact wording of the disclaimer. It took the projectionist two days and a magnifying glass to discern what was written.

Things got worse. In December 1996, Gillian's book *Love You to Bits and Pieces* was published, claiming on its front cover to be "the true story that inspired *Shine*." Yet it went even further than *Shine* in creating a mythology around David and his family—myself included. I could hardly believe my eyes when I read David "quoted" as saying: "If Margaret didn't play well, oh God. She got punished severely. Father was cruel to her verbally and aggressively too. He used violence" (page 103).

Next came the publication of the screenplay in book format. Now it was clearer than ever that Hicks had not lived up to his assurances in his letter of January 6, 1989, that it was not his intention to be judgmental about my father. I read that Peter Helfgott was "menacing"; at one point his "eyes glow with anger in the darkness" (scene 54a); at another his "eyes glow with hostility" (scene 78), and so on.

For good measure, some of the cast backed up *Shine*'s assertions. For example, Geoffrey Rush told Andy Warhol's *Interview* magazine that "this film isn't about a guy playing the piano, it's about how easily you can f**k up your kids."

Shine began to receive award after award. At the Australian Film Institute awards in November 1996, it took nine prizes out of eleven nominations. It won Golden Globes. It won awards from the Screen Actors Guild, the New York Film Critics Circle, the Los Angeles Film Critics Association, the U.S. National Board of Review, the Writers Guild of America, and more. It won awards in film festivals in a host of cities (Fort Lauderdale, Aspen, Hawaii, and so on) and in many countries, including Canada, Italy, and Britain. Australia's arts minister Richard Alston praised the film as "dazzling."

My father was painted in negative terms in countless articles, not just film reviews but analysis and feature articles, and some even on the editorial and opinion pages of the world's leading newspapers, including the *New York Times*. An Internet search reveals, for example, that in a six-month period, forty-eight articles and letters to the editor concerning or mentioning *Shine* appeared in the *Los Angeles Times* alone. Many papers carried profiles of the real-life David. "His father disowned him at the age of nineteen," stated one in the London *Sunday Times*. While the film's disclaimer is buried beyond recognition, full-page ads appeared in the papers saying the film was an "utterly extraordinary true story." Another ad said David was "driven to breaking point by . . . an abusive father."

Then came the big one, the Oscars, in late March 1997. I was extremely tense. *Shine* had been nominated for seven awards—including Best Director for Hicks, Best Picture, Best Actor, and Best Screenplay. One of the first awards of the evening was for Best Supporting Actor. When Cuba Gooding Jr. triumphed over the German actor Armin Mueller-Stahl, who played my father, I cried. I said to myself "Thank God," over and over again. "Sorry, Mr. Mueller-Stahl. I have nothing against you personally, but I'm sure you understand." But later in the ceremony, when Glenn Close said that *Shine* is the "true story" of David Helfgott, I flinched. When she went on to say that he "had survived *decades* of shock treatment," I didn't know whether to laugh or cry. I thought: The myth just grows and grows.

16

DRAMATIC DISTORTIONS IN *SHINE*

Shine is a film purporting to be a true story, but it is in fact riddled with errors and inaccuracies. I have mentioned some of these in previous chapters and do not propose reiterating them all in detail. Nevertheless there are some points on which I would like to elaborate. They concern both the film and the official screenplay—which differs from the version finally shot because some scenes were cut out of the film at the last moment, partly as a result of the increasing volume of the Helfgott family's protests. However, these scenes remain in the screenplay that is on sale at bookstores throughout the world, including my local bookstore here in Israel. This screenplay was published some months after the film's release, and is likely to be read by film buffs, students, and those interested in finding out more about David's life. In his introduction to the book, the screenwriter Jan Sardi claims, in what sounds to me like Orwellian double-talk, that the story of *Shine* "remains faithful to the essence of the biographical facts."

My father's role as the villain of the piece is built around several different themes. One of the first to be introduced is the idea that he regarded winning as all-important. In fact, my father never stressed winning, only doing one's best. Almost from the beginning, *Shine* conjures up an atmosphere of fear and dread around David's failure to win piano competitions. The character representing me says: "He lost. Now we'll cop it," while David walks several steps behind Peter, as if in disgrace. The words in the screenplay (scene 8) go even further. "Margaret" says: "Now we'll all cop it. Damn you, David Helfgott," which I, of course, never said. References to "winning" are sprinkled throughout the film. For example, David says: "Gotta win, gotta win" or something similar at several points (words that are not always in the screenplay). Sometimes the idea of winning at all costs has been used in juxtaposition with scenes that take place in the psychiatric hospital—which led several film reviewers to link David's mental illness with the supposed emphasis my father put on coming first—"a determination that David succeed at any cost," as the *New York Times* critic Janet Maslin put it in her review.

The theme of my father's alleged violent nature is introduced gradually. In scene 9, he knocks the chess pieces to the floor in the middle of a game, and then orders a frightened David to pick them up. In the words of the screenplay, Peter at this point "slams his fist on the small table," setting the stage for his later aggressive behavior. At the same time he says, "Margaret! I told you, tell your friends not to come." Needless to say, this incident never occurred, nor did my father ever prevent any of us going out with friends or having them to visit.

When in the film, Ben Rosen comes to our house to offer his services as a music teacher, my father not only refuses but is hostile to this stranger (scene 11 of the screenplay states: "Peter does not accept the proffered handshake by Rosen"). Later, when my father reluctantly takes David to Rosen's house, the scene is accompanied by ominous music. After an exchange at the door in which Rosen does not invite Peter in, Rosen agrees to teach David and then slams the door in Peter's face. Then, at a concert, "Rosen catches Peter looking. Neither hides their contempt." As I have explained earlier in this book, Frank Arndt, the real-life figure on whom the character of Rosen is modeled, had an excellent relationship with my father.

The first serious act of violence in the film is when Peter enters the bathroom, discovers excreta in David's bath, and hits him nine times with a towel, while saying, "To shit in the bath. You disgusting animal," repeating the word "animal" three times. At the end of the beating we see water dripping off the walls. The screenplay, scene 50, adds even more color. It reads: "The attack . . . continues across his bare back, his head . . . water runs down the walls like blood"—clearly implying that my father's beating caused David to bleed. I find this scene not only offensive to my father, but humiliating to my brother. In reality, while David did mess himself as a child, he never excreted in the bath, and my father certainly didn't flay him with a towel.

David's beating at home before he goes to London is the next violent incident. The film depicts a lengthy and disturbing scene showing Peter brutally beating his son, pummeling him over and over until he has to be pulled off by his family. The screenplay describes this over four pages and four scenes (78 to 81): I have outlined much of the dialogue earlier, in Chapter 8, but the stage directions of the screenplay leave the reader no room to doubt what a brute "my father" was: "Peter comes at David like a lumbering bear . . . Peter slaps David around the head knocking his glasses off . . . Peter gives Suzie a backhand . . . Peter throws David across the room. Margaret intervenes . . . Peter picks up a chair and throws it against the wall . . . Peter has David in a headlock, choking him . . . Rachel bashes [Peter's] arms with her fists trying to get him to let go of David who can't breathe. Margaret tries to pull Peter away . . . Margaret says 'I'll get the police' . . . David wipes his bloody nose . . . Rachel holds the girls, all crying."

As I have said before, there was an argument between my father and my brother, witnessed by all of us. It was unpleasant, but there was no violence. My whole family told Hicks that this scene is completely fictitious. Realizing that he could face legal action, he removed some elements, such as my father hitting Suzie, and "Margaret" saying "I'll get the police," though these remain in the screenplay.

As David leaves the house, the fictitious Peter announces: "Don't make me do it!"—a peculiar enough statement in itself—and then he proceeds to burn David's scrapbooks and other material. We see the reflection of the fire glowing in Peter's glasses. As the screenplay says (scene 82): "Music scores burn, schoolbooks, David's clothes . . . Peter throws another pile on, stokes the flames. Burning in the fire is the scrapbook—images of young David surrender to the flames." Nothing of this sort ever occurred. It sent shivers down my spine to see images so reminiscent of the Nazi burning of Jewish books in 1933, when over one million books were incinerated in public bonfires in Berlin's Opera House square and other locations, solely because their authors were Jewish.

My father is also shown returning David's letters. David sits at a table, with bottles of pills next to him, recording a tape to Katherine Susannah Pritchard. He says: "I wrote to Daddy. He didn't write back." The camera then moves to a bundle of letters marked "Return to Sender." David takes a tablet from one of the bottles and swallows it. Here again the juxtaposition clearly implies that a cruel father is driving poor David to medication. In his introduction to the screenplay, Jan Sardi specifically says that his aim was to allow "the audience to participate by having to fill it in for themselves" and that he wants to allow "visuals to tell the story" as well as dialogue. As I have explained in Chapter 9, we still have these letters—all of which were read, answered, and kept—but cannot reprint them since Gillian holds the copyright.

There are many scenes in *Shine* that portray David's close relationships with Pritchard and with his music professor Cecil Parkes; so much so that the two of them assume quasiparental roles in David's life. This has the effect of making my father and mother appear neglectful and unloving as parents.

Parkes is portrayed as warm and fatherlike. In the film (though not in the screenplay) Parkes says to David, "Come on, my boy," and takes him out to visit what appears to be a museum, pointing things out to him in a fatherly way—in much the same manner, in fact, as my father actually did. Parkes and David sing a duet together as they walk along merrily.

At one point David even addresses Parkes as "Daddy." In scene 121, Parkes sits next to David at the piano and looks genuinely concerned. He asks: "What on earth is the problem?" David says: "If you do something wrong can you be punished for the rest of your life?" (alluding to my father's entirely fictional "I won't let anyone destroy this family" speech). Parkes says: "David, listen to me," and David replies: "Yes, Daddy, sorry. Mustn't make you angry, not another angry lion."

In the screenplay, the scenes with Parkes have stage directions such as "Light pours in" (scene 112). Hicks has even put my real-life father's own words about music into Parkes's mouth. In scene 123, Parkes says to David: "Once you've done it [music] no one can ever take it away from you."

As well as falsely depicting my father as a tyrant and a bully, *Shine* totally negates my mother's role in David's life. If Cecil Parkes is a quasifather figure, then Katherine Pritchard is a quasimother. David plays for Pritchard, sits next to her, and engages in mother/sonlike dialogue. For example, in scene 63, he says: "Tell me a story, Katherine. What story is it today?"

In the film version, Pritchard has a framed photo of the teenage David on her mantelpiece; her house is warm and comforting, in sharp contrast to the cold and loveless atmosphere with which my parents' house is shrouded. Later on, David is shown sending tapes from London to Pritchard, but not to his own mother. Pritchard kisses and cuddles David. At one point, David asks her (scene 75) what her father was like, thus inviting comparison between families. In scene 72, Pritchard listens to David playing "the Rach 3," and then she looks at his photo and says, "Bravo, David."

Why doesn't Hicks have my mother saying "Bravo, David"? Why doesn't he show my mother reading David stories, as she did so often when he was young?

Katherine Pritchard's caring, motherly qualities are contrasted with my mother's sullen appearances at the kitchen sink. In the film, my mother is constantly grimy and involved in some household chore. She virtually ignores her children, and practically the only communication between her and my father is when they snap at each other. This is the complete opposite of my mother's true disposition. In reality, she and David have always been close.

A few months ago, Marta Kaczmarek, the actress who plays my mother in *Shine,* stumbled across Leslie performing the violin in a Perth market. She approached him and actually apologized profusely for the hurt and harm that have been caused to him by what she now knows to have been an utterly fictitious piece of cinema.

It is not only my poor mother who is portrayed as drab and unloving. The whole Helfgott home is painted with dull colors and the mood is always somber, transmitting a feeling of pervading darkness with little communication among its occupants. The action that takes place in the house is accompanied by doom-laden music and fearful glances, especially when my father enters—quite the opposite of how it really was. In the essay printed at the end of the screenplay, Hicks talks of the lighting in the film. He says: "We had to take the film into some very dark places, and chart the character's journey through that darkness, and out into the light again. And we agreed—let's not be frightened by shadows, dark corners, and corridors."

In addition to more direct methods of character definition, visual imagery is much used in *Shine*. It is often raining in the scenes involving my father or scenes when David has been abandoned. This is in spite of the fact that in reality Perth has a very sunny climate.

After the false scene in which David collapses upon completing "the Rach 3," the film moves straight into showing David receiving ECT treatment. ("His glasses are put on a metal tray. Electrodes are placed on his temples. The ECT dial is turned up.") To the best of my knowledge, David never actually received ECT. The film then shows a pale and gaunt David calling my father from a phone booth. When I saw the film in a theater in Perth, the scene in which Peter puts the phone down on David without replying after David says, "Daddy, I'm home. Daddy, hello, Daddy," induced a member of the audience to shout out "bas-

tard." Peter then draws the blinds down sharply, symbolizing his rejection of his son. As I have explained,
in reality we had no phone, David moved straight
back home and actually wrote to all kinds of people,
such as Professor Callaway. Many of them would
have talked to Hicks to confirm this.

But Hicks isn't done with my father yet. He continues to insult him even after he is dead. I have already discussed the offensive graveyard scene in
Chapter 13, when David says he feels "nothing." In
the screenplay, this scene (194) ends with Gillian
saying "Bravo" and then "laughing" before the joyous singing of "Funiculi, Funicula" in the background. All this, of course, contrasts starkly with the
tribute David actually paid his father in the local
newspaper, in letters, at the funeral, and in person
to myself and others.

There is a further point I would like to make on behalf of my former sister-in-law, Claire. One of the ma-
licious things said about her in Gillian's book is that
she stole the medal David won in London. This is
complete nonsense—David himself told us when he
arrived back in Perth almost a year before he married
Claire that he left the medal in London. But in the
film, there is an unexplained and surreal scene in
which my father visits David one last time, after
David has already started playing at Riccardo's/
Moby's. The real David began performing there in
1983, eight years after my father's death. In the film,
"Dad" places a gold medal around David's neck
(scene 184), before he walks away, a lonely figure
swallowed up by the night. This not only falsely suggests that we still had the medal, but also implies that

my father had been alive all this time and had not visited David, who has previously been referred to as a
"stray dog."

There are further scenes in the screenplay, which
don't appear in the film, that reinforce the idea that
David didn't care for his father. In scene 193, David
says he can't shed "any tears for the man of steel"
(which is how my father is referred to earlier in the
screenplay). In scene 190, David is dreaming, then
sees his father and wakes up "in a sweat."

Another scene that appears in the screenplay
(scene 48) but not in the film, shows Peter smashing
a milk bottle before hitting my mother. In real life,
there was an incident in Suzie's youth when she
dropped a milk bottle and it smashed, and another
occasion, outlined in Chapter 3, where I used a milk
bottle to put out the fire I accidentally caused in our
Melbourne flat. Is Hicks playing around with the facts
of our lives to create his own little fantasies? And then
passing off these fantasies as the truth, regardless of
whose lives are damaged in the process?

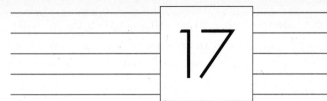

CHEAPENING THE HOLOCAUST

Although *Shine* is ostensibly a film about music, family relationships, and the struggle against mental illness, the Holocaust lurks in the background like a dark shadow. For those sensitive to it, the references to the Nazi genocide of European Jews that Hicks and his screenwriter, Jan Sardi, have embedded in the film are unmistakable. My parents lost family members in the Holocaust and this aspect of the film has affected me very deeply.

There is one particularly appalling remark in *Shine* that relates to me personally. Shortly after one of my father's fictional beatings of my brother, my character, Margaret, says: "This house is like a concentration camp" (scene 54). Although cut from the film, it remains in the published screenplay. Even Hicks and Sardi appear to have had last-minute jitters about putting it on screen—no doubt fearing that it might cause me to take out an injunction against the film. Yet they have had no such compunction about leaving it in the screenplay to be analyzed and devoured by unwitting students of film, drama, and Holocaust studies throughout the world. The notion that anyone who lost relatives in the Holocaust, or who has relatives who are concentration camp survivors, would say such a thing is repugnant.

I spoke about this to Professor Yehuda Bauer of the Hebrew University and of the Yad Vashem Holocaust Museum and Memorial in Jerusalem, who is arguably the world's leading expert on the Holocaust. In his words: "Anyone who could write such a line, who could make such a comparison to a normal or even to a seminormal household, obviously has no idea what a concentration camp is."

To make it clear just what an odious comparison was put into my mouth, and to demonstrate the vileness of the way in which Hicks and Sardi play with the Holocaust at many other points in *Shine,* I want to explain a little of the background of what did happen to my family in Czestochowa, Poland. Jews have lived in Poland for almost a thousand years and made an enormous contribution to the development of industry, commerce, and the arts throughout the country, as well as establishing social, educational, and charitable institutions. Czestochowa, with its flourishing Jewish community, was no exception.

When World War II broke out, on September 1, 1939, there were 28,486 Jewish men, women, and children living in Czestochowa. Two days later, on September 3, the German army entered the town and the very next day—later referred to as "Bloody

Monday"—a pogrom was organized, in which many hundreds of Jews were brutally murdered. A second pogrom was carried out on Christmas Day 1939, and Czestochowa's great synagogue was set ablaze. But worse was to follow for the town's Jews. In August 1940, about 1,000 young men between the ages of eighteen and twenty-five were sent to a forced labor camp in Cieszanow, near Lublin. Practically all of them perished. Many Jews from other parts of western Poland were uprooted from their communities and forced by the Nazis to move—temporarily—to Czestochowa, and the city's Jewish population swelled by several thousand. On April 9, 1941, the Nazis established a ghetto in the town, an area into which all the Jews were herded. On August 23, after it was filled to bursting point, it was sealed off and the population was left inside to endure starvation and disease.

In 1942, Yom Kippur, the Jewish Day of Atonement and the holiest day in the Jewish calendar, fell on September 22. The Germans chose this day to launch a large-scale *"aktion"* against the ghetto. By October 5, around 39,000 Jews had been deported to Treblinka concentration camp, fifty miles northeast of Warsaw, where they were murdered in gas chambers.

Originally built as a forced labor camp for political prisoners, Treblinka had been rebuilt in June 1942 and fully equipped with gas chambers and crematoria in preparation for its role in the genocide. In Treblinka, the Jews of Czestochowa joined Jews transported from all over Poland and Nazi-occupied Europe. Upon arrival in this hellhole, the vast majority were stripped naked and gassed. By August the following year, when a mass escape took place in which inmates overpowered and killed their SS guards, about 900,000 Jews had been killed at Treblinka. After Auschwitz, Treblinka is the second largest site of mass murder in history. Following the uprising, there were severe reprisals and the camp was dismantled in October 1943. Today the only trace that remains of Treblinka are thousands of shards of broken stone that lie on the spot where the camp once stood.

The Jews remaining in the camp at the time of its dissolution were moved to other camps where most were killed by shooting, gassing, hanging, electrocution, and lethal injection, or simply left to rot through disease and exhaustion. Others were used as slave labor, or subjected to sadistic torture dressed up as "medical experimentation."

Most people nowadays have some idea of the Holocaust from books and films such as Steven Spielberg's *Schindler's List*. But even Spielberg's film fails truly to convey the depths of depravity of the crimes perpetrated against the Jews. As one of the survivors of the real Schindler transports said of the film: "*Schindler's List* had no hangings. The dogs wore muzzles; audiences didn't see them gnawing men's genitals and women's breasts. Spielberg's storm troopers refrained from swinging infants by their feet into brick walls, smashing their skulls like melons."

After many of their number had been sent to Treblinka, only around 6,500 Jews remained in the Czestochowa ghetto, which was then allocated smaller borders. On January 4, 1943, about 300 men in the ghetto, calling themselves the Jewish Fighting

Organization, unsuccessfully tried to launch an uprising. The next day the Nazis shot 250 children and old
people as punishment. In June, the remaining Jews
were transferred to two slave labor camps set up at
the Hasag factories in Czestochowa that were privately owned by a German industrialist. On July 20,
1943, some 500 prisoners from these camps who had
"served their purpose" were taken to the town's
Jewish cemetery and executed. Before evacuating
Czestochowa on January 17, 1945, the Germans managed to deport almost 6,000 prisoners from the Hasag
camps to the concentration camps at Buchenwald,
Gross-Rosen, and Ravensbrueck. (One of those, then
aged seven, who worked at Czestochowa's labor
camp and subsequently survived Buchenwald, is
Yisrael Lau, now Israel's Chief Rabbi.)

By the end of the war, only about 2,000 of Czestochowa's prewar Jewish population of almost 30,000
remained alive. Among those who had been murdered were my mother's two sisters and all my father's immediate family, including his sisters Miriam,
Na'acha, and Rivka and his brothers Zelig and
Abraham. Among those who survived were my
mother's brother Johnny (liberated from Buchenwald)
and her stepmother Bronia (liberated from Bergen-
Belsen). Zelig Lewcowitz, a cousin of my father
(whom I used to visit at his home in Tel Aviv until he
passed away a short time ago), went back to
Czestochowa in 1945 and could find no one else of
our family alive. Today, when nearly all other Polish
Jews have left Poland, there are still small organizations of Czestochowa-born Jews active in Israel, the
United States, Canada, Argentina, and France. In

Czestochowa itself hardly any signs exist that a half century ago Jews comprised 30 percent of the population. The Jewish museum, for example, is now a school; and a big industrial factory has been built around the Jewish cemetery, making it impossible to see it from the street without going through the factory.

Incredibly, some of the Jews who managed to survive the death camps were killed in Poland in the two years after Germany's surrender. For example, in the town of Kielce, not far from Czestochowa, 42 Jewish concentration camp survivors were killed by a Polish mob in July 1946.

A whole world had been destroyed. Clearly, for the survivors, Poland was no place to rebuild their shattered lives, and the vast majority fled the country, going mainly to Israel (or Palestine, as it was known before independence was declared in 1948). Bronia and Johnny came to Melbourne in 1946, part of an estimated 18,000 Jewish Holocaust survivors who moved to Australia at the end of the war. Even now, the German Chancellor, Helmut Kohl, who visited Australia in May 1997, is still negotiating over compensation payments for survivors living there.

After the war, Franz Stangl, the Austrian commandant who ran Treblinka (and before that Sobibor) escaped, aided, unbelievably, by the Red Cross and the Vatican. He went first to Syria and then moved to Brazil in 1951, where he registered at the Austrian consulate under his own name and worked as an engineer for Volkswagen in São Paulo. In 1967, he was tracked down by the Nazi hunter Simon Wiesenthal, extradited to Germany, and convicted in a Düsseldorf court of the murder of 900,000 people—including my mother's two little sisters and most of my father's family. He was sentenced to life imprisonment and died in prison in 1971.

The Holocaust was "the most horrible crime committed in the whole history of the world," as Winston Churchill described it, and it traumatized Jews and many others. But neither my father nor my mother had personally experienced the hell of the concentration camps—contrary to what Scott Hicks implies when playing around with my family's lives. To portray my father as a brute and then explain this behavior by insinuating that he was a concentration camp survivor is not only a terrible slur on my father but highly insulting to all Holocaust survivors and their families.

The very idea, so strongly suggested by Hicks, of my father, the supposed Holocaust survivor, adopting the manner of his persecutors, is grotesque. In the film, the Holocaust is strongly evoked by the use of images—barbed wire cuts across my father's face as he nails shut the garden fence to keep his children's friend out; scrapbooks are burned, there is a mark on Peter's forearm. To add insult to injury, Hicks cast a German actor with a strong German accent to play my Polish father. In the eyes of many, my father thus became a German Jew: "David Helfgott's mind was knocked off-kilter by a despotic German-Jewish father," said the *Financial Times* of London, January 2, 1997.

This undercurrent of Holocaust themes has deeply hurt me both personally and publicly. Without exception, after they saw *Shine,* friends and acquaintances of mine presumed that they "knew" from the film that my father was a concentration camp survivor. They were astounded when I said he wasn't. For those with even a little knowledge of the Holocaust the signs in the film are obvious.

As a columnist in the Philadelphia *Jewish Exponent* wrote to his great surprise in the March 20, 1997, issue: "A recent article in the *New York Times* revealed that the real-life Helfgotts were not Holocaust survivors. They left Poland before Hitler's invasion. This is not a trivial detail to Holocaust survivors, who are rightly sensitive about comparisons between their memories and those who watched from a distance."

My friends, presuming like everyone else that *Shine* was true, had trouble believing me. "What about when he showed the concentration camp number to one of his daughters?" was a constant refrain. "What about the barbed wire?" Some shuddered when they recalled the "nighttime burning of the documents, the flames," just like Nazi Germany purging itself of Jewish "influences." The nineteenth-century German-Jewish poet Heinrich Heine was right when he said: "Where books are burned, human beings are also destined to be burned." To make sure we get the point, we see the photo of "young David" surrendered to the flames. When Peter throws David's material into the stove, the reflection of the fire flickering across his glasses, an image of the crematoria where the bodies of Jews—including many of my relatives— were incinerated is conjured up.

Friends also say: "I remember when your father beat David in the bath in the first part of the film—so it gave me shivers when David looked up from his

bath in a later scene and saw clouds of steam ema-
nating from the shower nozzle head." It is no accident that in this scene the camera lingers for a
moment too long on the shower nozzle and on the
steam. It bears a close resemblance to the beginnings
of gassing scenes in Holocaust films.

These powerful visual images are combined with
many suggestions in the dialogue. The word "survivor" is used repeatedly throughout the film. For example, the character of David says: "To survive, to
survive undamaged" in scene 2; Peter says: "In this
world only the fit survive." It is the dialogue put in
David's mouth that essentially also reinforces the
Holocaust theme. He declares: "You see, Daddy's
daddy was religious, vee-eery religious, very strict;
and a bit of a meanie. But he got exterminated, didn't
he, so God didn't help him. Whooahhh" (scene 4); or
"The Pole-popolski. Like Daddy and his family before
they were concentrated" (scene 18). Even in the
halfway house David's character is muttering: "The
weak get crushed like insects, like grasshoppers."

Another example of Hicks and Sardi mixing dialogue and visual imagery is scene 25 when my father
says: "You are very lucky to have a family," and then
immediately his face appears over the corrugated
iron fence with a strand of barbed wire running
across the top.

We can see, by comparing the screenplay with the
film version, that Hicks is deliberately changing the
facts as he goes along. Scene 30 of the screenplay
says my father had a SCAR on the palm of his HAND
("Peter extends his hand . . . to reveal a scar"). But in
the film he rolls up his sleeve and my young sister

looks goggle-eyed at a MARK on my father's FORE-
ARM at exactly the place where concentration camp
inmates were tattooed with their identity numbers.
Then, having muffled his next words that refer to the
scar, so as to render them barely audible (a point
picked up by a reviewer for the *New York Times*), my
father regains his normal clear voice: "No one can
hurt me! Because in this world only the fit survive.
The weak get crushed like insects."

The director was fully aware that my father was not
a concentration camp survivor, yet created a film with
the aforementioned imagery. Not surprisingly, newspaper commentators and film critics were misled by
Hicks's hideous Holocaust implications. "Scott Hicks
tells a true story and tells it deftly . . . Darkness enters
with Armin Mueller-Stahl's father . . . a concentration
camp survivor" (London *Times,* January 2, 1997);
"The real-life Helfgott . . . was for more than a decade
lodged in mental institutions and kept from playing . . . Peter drives his son relentlessly . . . fueled by
his Holocaust experiences" (*Chicago Tribune,*
November 27, 1996). The most awful things were
written in reviews, reaching an audience that may not
themselves even have seen the film. The critic for
London's influential newspaper, the *Evening
Standard* (January 2, 1997), described my father as "a
character only slightly less lovable than Himmler: yet
he's suffered and survived the death camps . . . [he
comes out] a mental and physical bully . . . and I can't
forgive him because of his morally privileged status
as a Holocaust survivor." On the other side of the
Atlantic, reviewers were drawing much the same conclusions. *Time* magazine (December 2, 1996) said my

father speaks to his son in a "führer-knows-best-tone."

Just when I thought nothing could possibly upset me further, even more horrible reviews appeared. "Stahl had the juiciest part of all as Helfgott's gestapo-like father," wrote Gary Wolcott in the *Tri-City Herald* (Pasco, Washington) on March 14, 1997, under the headline "Film Shines Light on Effects of Child Abuse." Elaine Dutka, writing her pre-Oscar roundup in the *Los Angeles Times* in March 1997, quoted acting coach Larry Moss as saying: "Mueller-Stahl [in *Shine*] was unafraid to let the audience dislike him. He showed the monster inside with fangs and blood intact. The actor was almost Hitleresque in his body language." This review not only compares my father to Hitler but also imbues him with a vampirelike persona, with overtones of some hideous creature straight out of a medieval purgatory painting. It reminded me of some of the vilest anti-Semitic drawings produced by early German *volk* (folk) literature, and of the virulent anti-Jewish propaganda films the Nazis used to influence the public in their crusade against the Jews.

My blood also ran cold when I came across the idea that my real-life father was so evil that he did not deserve to be genetically linked to David. Peter Helfgott "does not, by spiritual measures, belong on David's family tree," wrote Brent Northup in the *Helena Independent Record* (Helena, Montana) on March 14, 1997.

Some reviewers directly suggest that the house that I grew up in had the atmosphere of a concentration camp. For example, Bill Hanna writing in the

Intelligencer (a daily newspaper in Wheeling, West Virginia) on March 15, 1997, says, "David's fanatically strict father runs his household much like a prison camp."

Sometimes I was able to correct journalists before the damage was done. Thane Rosenbaum of the *New York Times* called me while writing a feature article on *Shine*. He was taken aback when I told him that my father was not in fact a Holocaust survivor. He wrote about what was for him an astonishing revelation in his subsequent article, on March 2, 1997, stating that "each of these images [in *Shine*] points to the conclusion that Peter Helfgott was a Holocaust survivor."

From the most highbrow publications to the popular magazines the story was the same: in a sickening role reversal the "victim" became the "aggressor." "Mr. Hicks offers us the Holocaust-surviving father, unwittingly imposing his tragic suffering on the next generation . . . He damages his son's health and art. Have the sins of the fathers been visited upon the sons?" (Kyle Pruett in the *New York Times,* November 17, 1996). "[Helfgott is] controlled by his loving but bullheaded and physically abusive father, a victim of the Holocaust" (*Cosmopolitan* magazine, December 1996).

By the time of the Oscars, Leslie and I were giving interviews on major television stations, such as CNN, trying to get the truth across. Some commentators saw these interviews and realized what Hicks was up to. "Hicks is certainly playing Holocaust head games with the *Shine* audience," wrote Gerald Peary in the Rhode Island paper *The Providence Phoenix* (April 4,

1997). It wasn't enough for Hicks to turn my father into a monster, he had, as one reviewer said, to make my father "a monster with an explanation."

I didn't know whether to laugh or cry when I read Hicks, quoted in the *New York Times* on the role the Holocaust plays in *Shine:* "This subject is still an open wound for some people," he said, "and I didn't want to trample on profound sensitivities by being offensive."

I wish I could say that Hicks's offensive treatment of Jews was restricted to the Holocaust. But his entire treatment of Judaism and Christianity raises very disturbing questions. Whereas the Jewish-related themes in *Shine* are dealt with in a negative, gloomy way throughout most of the film, at the end—coinciding with the entrance of love and happiness into David's life—Christianity and Christian symbols are suddenly introduced, accompanied by bright blue skies and uplifting choral music. In several unexplained scenes and camera shots, large crosses appear and we see David in church. If the character of David has not quite become a Christian, Hicks seems to want us to know he has at any rate been saved by Christianity.

There is of course absolutely nothing wrong with using lots of light, love, and music during Christian scenes. Both Christianity and Judaism can be uplifting religions. But what is so disturbing is the way Hicks is misusing Christianity as a means of portraying Jews and Judaism in a negative light. Hicks's message seems to be that the Jews destroyed David, but his rehabilitation and later success are attributed to Christian kindness. Whereas there is often dark and foreboding music when my father appears on screen, when David leaves the hospital toward the end of the film (scene 146), he is accompanied by Vivaldi's "Gloria"—symbolizing the ultimate salvation. The music builds up over five scenes, culminating in the church (scene 151). Whereas in scene 9 of the screenplay, a picture of a "stern rabbi" hangs on the wall of the sinister Helfgott house, suddenly in scene 148, "A framed picture of Christ hangs on the wall," as the screenplay puts it. This would all be fine except that in real life David is not a Christian; he is a proud Jew who has chosen, for example, to donate some proceeds from his 1997 world concert tour to Jewish charities.

Shine would have it differently. The motherly figure of Katherine Susannah Pritchard says of David (scene 65): "You are Krishna, Christ, and Dionysus," omitting his Jewish background. In contrast, David's real Jewish mother is portrayed as a sullen drudge in the kitchen and as "helpless" with regard to her poor stricken son. There is almost nothing positive about the Jewish Helfgott family in the film. Even on the rare occasions when love is expressed, a suffocating feeling accompanies it. Whenever there is violence, shouting, or swearing, it is in Yiddish, the language of European Jews. For example, scene 80 of the screenplay states, "Rachel screams in Yiddish"; or scene 40, "Peter curses again in Yiddish."

There is also implied Jewish prejudice against non-Jews; Peter only responds to Ben Rosen after Rosen speaks Yiddish, i.e., he warms up to him when he finds out that Rosen, too, is Jewish. This is ridiculous and not at all how my father was in real life. The real Frank Arndt wasn't Jewish. But his cinematic alter ego, Rosen, obviously is. I presume Hicks turned Arndt into a Jew because he didn't want a non-Jew to voice the completely false and anti-Semitic idea that Jews regard their religion as a money-spinner. When Rosen introduces the idea of a bar mitzvah, Peter says: "What?" Rosen replies: "David hasn't had his bar mitzvah." Peter then says: "Religion is nonsense," and Rosen replies: "It's also a gold mine if you know where to dig" (scene 24).

No, Mr. Hicks. Having a bar mitzvah is not a fund-raising scheme, but an educational exercise designed to instruct a young boy in his faith and culture, a ceremony with deep traditional and spiritual significance. In the synagogue scene, my father looks cold and his face wears an uncompromising and menacing expression. In the screenplay (scene 51) the words actually used are "David cowers." This is all in marked contrast to the later joyful expressions in church.

Shine's David is peculiarly uncomfortable with his Judaism. Nowhere is this more apparent than in the frivolous way in which he talks about the Holocaust and in his negative references to Israel—he dismisses it as merely "a battleground, a war zone; what a bore." In the film, but not in the screenplay, David adds that Israel "just destroys everything really, doesn't it?" In reality my brother would never judge Israel by its often distorted, negative, simplistic, and arguably anti-Semitic television image.

In almost all the letters he has ever written me, David has said positive things about Israel. He repeatedly told me how much he wanted to visit Israel, and, after his visit, how much he enjoyed it. He calls

Israel "a beautiful country." In one letter, he says "those people in Masada must have had tons of courage—they had the right spirit," referring to the Jews in the ancient hilltop fortress who, two millennia ago, committed suicide rather than surrender to the Romans. He talks in some detail about wanting to go to the concerts that are held in ancient amphitheaters in Israel, and to the Mann Concert Auditorium in Tel Aviv. He talks about all the archaeological and historical sites he wants to visit. He says how he hopes Israeli athletes will perform well in the Olympic games. In one letter, he recalls how horrified he was when Palestinian terrorists murdered Israeli athletes at the 1972 Munich Olympics. He says he remembers how his music lesson that day was canceled as a mark of respect. Since the 1970s, David has been fascinated by Israeli politics, giving me his opinion, in various letters, on politicians from David Ben-Gurion to Golda Meir.

David has always been proud of his Jewish roots. In one letter to me he writes that although he is not religious he "thoroughly enjoys reading about the Talmud and Jewish religious writings." In another he says he is "looking forward to going to the Liberal *schule* [the Yiddish word for synagogue] on Friday." He tells me of the "fascinating books" about European Jewish history and the Holocaust that he has been reading.

David has performed at fund-raising concerts for Jewish and Israeli causes. He played, for example, in Melbourne in 1987 for the Friends of the Israel Philharmonic Orchestra, and in Sydney for the Women's Zionist Organization. So why is Hicks so eager to show David emerging out of the Jewish darkness into the Christian light? Unfortunately, to people familiar with classic anti-Semitic motifs, the themes of the Jew as responsible for his own misfortune and of Christian redemption are all too familiar.

The London *Evening Standard* reviewer picked up on this: "Lynn Redgrave (Gillian) plays the astrologer who plucks the damaged boy from the pressure-cooker Jewish household into the curative stewpot of a Christian environment—the faith is explicitly emphasized. I suspect the cheerleaders for the film, which is being heavily touted for Oscar honors, have an agenda of their own that I don't entirely share."

The real life Gillian, too, raises some disturbing questions about her opinions of Jews in her book, *Love You to Bits and Pieces*. For example, within the course of five pages (49 to 53), the words "rich Jews" appear eight times. (For instance, the line "he had to throw himself at the mercy of those rich Jews" is used on page 49.) The term also appears later in the book. But she doesn't use the term "rich Christian" or "rich Gentile" when we read, for example, about Russell Smith of Camon Mining who gave David $10,000 in the late 1980s.

She falsely claims that my paternal grandfather was a rabbi and that my father chased his rabbi father around the table trying to cut off his beard with a pair of scissors. To ascribe such disrespectful behavior to my father is preposterous. Again, this has overtones of the Nazi period—the Nazis forced many Jews to cut off their beards publicly in the streets, while humiliating and insulting them.

I had sincerely hoped that the lines about Jews,

and the Holocaust, both in *Love You to Bits and Pieces* and in *Shine,* were the result of extreme insensitivity and ignorance, rather than of ill will and prejudice. However, all the evidence leaves me and others no choice but to conclude that the impression received by the majority of filmgoers was the one Hicks intended to convey.

18

MEDICAL ORGANIZATIONS ATTACK *SHINE*

One source of support in my campaign against *Shine* has been the medical profession. Doctors and medical organizations have been dismayed by the way Hicks's film suggests that "bad parenting" can be the cause of serious mental illness. This idea is a misconception made popular in the 1960s. Unfortunately it is still widespread. Following a torrent of newspaper articles that stated that my "brutish" father "caused" David's illness, various medical bodies felt they had to speak out. Though it was obvious to psychiatric experts that *Shine* was playing around with the truth while purporting to be based on fact, they were concerned that this was not obvious to millions of ordinary filmgoers. They feared that thousands of innocent families of mentally ill people were being hurt by the false picture presented in *Shine*. As my family knows only too well, it is hard enough having to cope with the mental illness of a loved one without being blamed for it as well.

While the person suffering the illness is, of course, its main victim, families of the mentally ill can suffer terribly, too, as their time and patience are stretched to the limit and they are financially drained by the high costs of medical treatment.

While nobody attaches blame to a family when someone suffers from physical ailments such as kidney failure or a sore throat, when a person is mentally ill, there are those who are all too eager to find an easy scapegoat upon whom to heap blame. By doing so, they are not only revealing a lack of medical knowledge, but are demonstrating an inability to accept the reality: psychotic mental illness is in fact rooted in biological or physical factors such as chemical imbalance in the brain, and is often genetically determined.

Those who attempt to invent social causes for such illness may make remarks like "they spoiled him"; "they were too good to him"; "they neglected him"; "his mother went out to work and wasn't there when he came home from school"; "they didn't let him do his own thing"; "he went to the wrong school"; and so on. Even worse, the patient himself, not fully aware of what he is saying, may blame his own family.

Medical experts (as opposed to fanciful filmmakers) will tell you that "endogenous" mental illnesses— by which they mean schizophrenia, affective disorders, manic depression, and paranoia—are certainly not caused by bad parenting. In David's case the way blame has been assigned is even more unjust since there was no bad parenting. Like many families in similar situations we have done a great deal to look after David in terms of our time, our emotions, and our energy as well as money. While he was alive my father did more than anyone.

Yet *Shine* would have it otherwise. For example, scene 143 of the screenplay reads as follows:

143. INT. PSYCHIATRIC HOSPITAL CORRIDOR. DAY

BERYL *walks along with a* NURSE.

BERYL: What goes on in his head?

NURSE: God only knows.

BERYL: Is he schizophrenic or something?

NURSE: No, he just lives in his own little world; no trouble at all.

BERYL: Poor lost soul.

NURSE: He could leave tomorrow, but he's got nowhere to go.

In one fell swoop, filmgoers and readers alike are misled both with regard to David's "invisible" family and to the seriousness of his illness.

David has been seen by various doctors who have all determined that his mental problems have a physiological basis. While the precise details of his medical records remain confidential, David and Gillian have given permission for his current psychiatrist, Dr. Susan Wynn, to make public the fact that he has been diagnosed as suffering from schizo-affective disorder, a form of psychosis related to schizophrenia. Dr. Wynn has discussed David's condition several times on television programs, such as *Witness* in Australia (August 6, 1996) and *The South Bank Show* in Britain (June 22, 1997). She has also confirmed that with a case such as this, the genetic component can be very significant.

Dr. Chris Reynolds, who looked after David in the early 1980s and had access to his Graylands Hospital medical records, has also publicly stated that David was treated for a schizophrenia-related illness (in the *Los Angeles Times,* November 17, 1996).

Yet Scott Hicks has a different diagnosis. At many points in the film, David's illness is put down to mere eccentricity, as he hops and skips around the psychiatric hospital in search of his "lost childhood." The pressure to win, which my fictional father constantly puts David under, is even alluded to in the mental hospital: for example, in scene 139, David tells the nurse "gotta win, gotta win"—the implication being that David is there because of his father's constant emphasis on "winning." In his introduction to the published screenplay, Hicks claims that this is "the story of a boy who is never allowed to grow up." No one stopped David from growing up. The "Production Background" at the back of the screenplay describes David as an "eccentric pianist" and an "endearing eccentric" and so on. The hereditary factors in the Helfgott family tree—the mental illnesses of my father's sister and his aunt—are conveniently omitted, thus paving the way for the blame to be laid on my father.

Gillian Helfgott has taken much the same approach. In her book, she does admit at one point that David has "a chemical imbalance in the brain," and tends to become "manic" when he doesn't take his medication, but this is rarely alluded to again. In newspaper and radio interviews, instead of explaining the nature of David's illness, she has consistently downplayed his medical diagnosis and asserted that David is just an "eccentric."

The fact is that David's illness exists completely independent of his environment. Although modern medicine has yet to determine precisely what causes such biological disorders, we do know that they commonly begin to manifest themselves in adolescence and then gradually develop, as happened in David's case. Often it develops so gradually that the family and even the person with the disease may not realize anything is wrong for a long period of time. Or sometimes, as in our case, relatives sense something is wrong, but have no idea as to its seriousness until an acute episode is experienced. Certainly, for me, it has been extremely painful to watch the personality changes that David has slowly undergone since he was a young teenager.

Dr. David Leonard, the director of psychiatry at Frankston Hospital in Victoria, Australia, is an expert on this disorder. He explains: "People with schizoaffective disorder will have both the symptoms of schizophrenia, and also the symptoms of bipolar disorder (manic depression). They may have manic episodes when they become extremely overactive, experience feelings of elation, and develop grandiose views of themselves. At other times the reverse may be the case and they will suffer severe depression. They will be profoundly unhappy, slowed up in their movements and unable to act . . . At other times they may believe themselves persecuted victims of complex conspiracies, a belief that may be confirmed by the presence of tormenting auditory hallucinations. These presentations are called paranoid and may be consistent with a capacity to continue to function reasonably in some spheres of their lives despite their delusions."

Yet the stigmas attached to mental illness are still largely rooted in society. Members of a patient's family can easily feel in some way to blame, or guilty about finding it hard to cope. These myths are put across with so much energy and power in *Shine* that almost without exception the critics got it wrong, blaming my brother's illness on my father's alleged brutality. And in doing so, since they were under the impression that *Shine* was essentially based on fact, they naturally made no distinction between the fictional Helfgotts and the real Helfgotts.

I had the pleasure of reading in various newspapers in the United States and elsewhere that David's mind "snapped because of intense performance pressure from his demanding, overprotective father"; that his "emotional torment under a domineering father led to schizophrenia"; that "after the way Peter Helfgott treats his son, it's no wonder David ended up as a nervous wreck . . . with mental problems." Yes, here he was, the "Holocaust Survivor . . . [who]

relentlessly pushed his talented pianist son to the brink of insanity." The speculation about Peter Helfgott's ability to cause chemical imbalances in the brain was occasionally so preposterous as to be laughable. One newspaper in Scotland didn't just blame the "stress which clearly existed between Peter and his son" for "David's mental illness" but even suggested that my father was "a hardline Stalinist" and this might have something to do with it.

Some papers got it spectacularly wrong. For example, the London *Sunday Times* said: "Despite the formidable task of being about two subjects—mental illness and music—that the cinema gets wrong on an almost annual basis, *Shine* gets both right." It was when the publicity surrounding *Shine* started spreading beyond Australia that many medical organizations felt the need to speak out in an attempt to counteract its harmful myth-making.

Dr. Margaret Leggatt, president of the World Schizophrenia Fellowship, and Barbara Hocking, executive director of SANE (the Schizophrenic Association of Australia), together began writing letters to newspapers; SANE urged its sister organizations, NAMI (the National Alliance for the Mentally Ill) in the United States and SANE in the United Kingdom, to do likewise.

"It is time that the myth of bad parenting or family arguments causing mental illness is put to rest," they wrote in letters published in November 1996 in *The Australian* and in *The (Melbourne) Age* (which had written that David "was battered psychologically by his father to the point of breakdown"). Leggatt and Hocking continued: "David Helfgott's story has made

public the plight of 180,000 families where someone
will have a schizophrenic illness. What a pity that the
filmmakers chose to make David's father the villain of
the piece. . . . If family members are portrayed by
filmmakers in cruel and fictitious scenarios, the blame
will continue. Fictionalization in films such as *Shine*
which are perceived by the community as true does
matter. It is inaccurate and unjust." (Much to the
amazement of Margaret Leggatt and Barbara Hocking,
Gillian went on a well-known Australian radio program, *Family Matters,* and said they had no right to
write to newspapers about her husband's illness and
this was none of their concern.)

Shine's actors have also, perhaps unwittingly, per-
petuated the myth of the film they had starred in.
Geoffrey Rush—who won the Oscar for Best Actor
for his role as David—told journalists: "This film is
about how easily you can f**k up your kids." Armin
Mueller-Stahl—whose role as my father also won him
an Oscar nomination—said: "Peter pushes his son to
be a great pianist. Because he's a very strong person,
a true survivor, he pushes far too hard, which ultimately destroys David."

SANE became so perturbed by the way these myths
were being spread by the hype surrounding *Shine*
that it issued a special briefing on the movie: "The
film's portrayal of David's father had rekindled the
untrue, inaccurate, and destructive myth that parental
and family behaviour caused psychotic mental illnesses such as schizo-affective disorder."

Barbara Hocking said: "This concerns us very much
in the mental health field as irresponsible comments
by public figures [such as Rush and Mueller-Stahl] fur-

ther reinforce the preexisting misconceptions. Scientific opinion accepts that psychotic illness does not develop unless there is an underlying biological predisposition.

"Scenes in *Shine*," she continued, "such as the one in David's London apartment, implying that the father's alleged rejection of David by returning his letters led him to overdose on medication, and the one in which it is stated that David's character is not really ill but is in hospital because he has nowhere to go, make our work much harder. It is irresponsible to suggest that someone would have been hospitalized and medicated just because he had nowhere else to go."

The medical inaccuracies in *Shine* have created such a stir that psychiatrists have even written papers in order to set the record straight. Under the title "Schizophrenia, Schizo-affective Disorders and *Shine*," Dr. David Leonard of the Frankston Hospital wrote:

"A film, of course, is never reality. But Geoffrey Rush's presentation of David Helfgott in *Shine* looks a lot like a disorganized presentation of schizophrenia. The character in the film has the typical jumbled thoughts, wildly inappropriate emotional responses, and lack of social judgment characteristic of the disorder. Fortunately for him, it all translates into a lovable zaniness that everyone finds appealing . . . It is a pity that the film chooses to seek out a villain in David Helfgott's father as the cause of the disorder. We do not know what causes schizophrenia, or similar disorders, but it seems quite clear that it is not a result of faulty upbringing. To blame a family for the illness is to double their pain. Not only must they bear the loss of their often promising and delightful children to this merciless illness, but they stand accused by others and by themselves of being the cause of the catastrophe. Families who have been touched by schizophrenia stand in need of our utmost kindness, support, and compassion, instead of such cruelty."

There was growing disquiet on the other side of the world, too. On January 11, 1997, the prestigious *British Medical Journal* published an article by Dr. Simon Wessely, from the department of psychology at King's College School of Medicine in London, entirely devoted to *Shine*. Under the title "Medicine and the Media—Mental Illness as Metaphor, Yet Again," Dr. Wessely wrote: "*Shine* repeats the error . . . that mental illness must have both a meaning and a cause. The roots of David's breakdown are laid firmly at the door of his father. The script comes straight out of those 1960s books on the schizophrenogenic family, replete with double binds, harsh discipline, overprotection, excessive love, and impossible expectations . . . a version of reality that is both inaccurate and patronizing."

American medical experts were also coming forward in an attempt to expose the myth. Patricia Backlar, senior scholar at the Center for Ethics in Health Care at Oregon Health Sciences University and author of the book *The Family Face of Schizophrenia,* wrote an opinion piece on *Shine* for the *Oregonian* of Portland, Oregon, on March 29, 1997. She said that if she had not known better, she "would believe that [Helfgott's] father had caused his son to become seriously mentally disordered." She felt that inherent within this film was "the evil implication that the father was powerful enough to cause his son to become seriously mentally disordered."

In a lengthy letter to the *New York Times* published on March 15, 1997, and entitled "*Shine* Depicts False View of Mental Illness," Dr. Kenneth Paul Rosenberg wrote: ". . . the most egregious misinformation in the film is the attribution of David's nervous breakdown to the cruelty of his father. Since cinema began, mental illness has been attributed to heartless parents. Most such films were produced during the middle of the century, when the idea was advanced by mental health professionals, particularly by psychoanalysts who saw the 'schizophrenogenic mother' as the evil root of all mental illness. Today we recognize that such theories added outrageous insult to severe injury."

He continues: "I worry about the impact of the film on the millions of individuals and families dealing with major mental illness. *Shine* . . . seems to continue a tradition of blaming parents for mental illnesses that rob their children of meaningful lives—illness that, to the best of our understanding, defies the logic of searching for human villains."

Another letter about *Shine* to the *New York Times* (March 30, 1997), printed under the headline "An Illness Rooted in Biology, Not Abuse," by Dr. Jonathan Segal of California, stated: "It is not appropriate to link David Helfgott's illness directly to . . . Peter Helfgott's terror . . . schizophrenia has strong biological roots . . . Most schizophrenics don't come from abusive homes, and most children in abusive homes don't develop schizophrenia." At least the message about schizophrenia was getting through, even if not the truth about my gentle father.

This is not just an issue for the Helfgott family. Honest discussion of mental illness remains taboo in many circles, and many people may not realize the extent to which it affects society. In Australia, around 20 percent of the population (3.5 million people) are affected by some form of mental illness at some time during their lives. In Britain, an estimated seven million people suffer from mental illness. According to the Schizophrenia Society of Canada, 250,000 Canadians will suffer from schizophrenia at some point in their lives. In the United States, too, about 1 percent of the population suffers from schizophrenia (according to research at Johns Hopkins University in Baltimore).

Nor is David alone among pianists. The celebrated British pianist John Ogden was engaged in a lifelong struggle against mental imbalance. Vladimir Horowitz—to whom David had been compared by his professor in London, Cyril Smith—was unable to perform for twelve years after suffering a nervous breakdown in 1953, at the age of forty-eight. Afterward, Horowitz, one of this century's greatest pianists, did resume his career but at a greatly diminished pace. And the Canadian pianist Glenn Gould had to give up live public performance at the age of thirty-two. (Gould would talk and sing to himself while playing, in a manner not unlike David's behavior in the last few years.)

Even *Shine*'s favorite musician, Rachmaninoff, himself suffered a nervous breakdown in 1897 and did not compose for several years until a prominent physician, Dr. Nikolai Dahl, used hypnosis and autosuggestion to bring him out of his despair. (To the best of my knowledge no one has made up a film about Rachmaninoff's father beating him into illness.)

Unfortunately, in spite of all this, the vast majority of newspaper commentary on *Shine* swallowed Hicks's version. Only a small minority of writers understood the games he was playing. One of these, Peter Rainer of the *New York Times,* hit the nail on the head when he said that *Shine* blames Peter Helfgott because "physiology doesn't play as well as Freud." Unfortunately, in making the kind of film he has created, Hicks was not just hurting the Helfgott family but seriously misleading the public and affecting millions of those touched by mental illness across the world.

19

DAVID'S 1997 WORLD TOUR: CLASSICAL MUSIC'S HOTTEST TICKET

He came, he played, he conquered." Thus began the review in the *Philadelphia Inquirer* of one of David's concerts on his 1997 world tour. It was about the only good review my poor brother got. In Australia, his concert was compared to "a freak show." In New Zealand, one critic said: "A Helfgott performance is like Beethoven on Prozac." In America, David's playing was described as "shapeless and utterly incoherent." A British newspaper said: "It was like watching a Muppet give a recital." His recital was "an exaggerated clatter," said another.

To coincide with the release of *Shine* in Australia, a concert tour was arranged for David. The whole Helfgott family, myself included, attended the first concert, a sellout performance at the Perth Concert Hall on August 31, 1996. When it became apparent that *Shine* would become a worldwide success, a lucrative world tour was hastily arranged, beginning in New Zealand in February 1997 and then taking David to some of the world's most distinguished musical venues.

It was a grueling schedule. In New Zealand my brother played six concerts in ten days; between each concert he changed location, skipping almost nightly from city to city and venue to venue. In March and April, David crisscrossed the United States, playing in the country's leading concert halls: the Boston Symphony Hall, New York's Avery Fisher Hall, Los Angeles's Dorothy Chandler Pavilion, San Francisco's Nob Hill Masonic Hall, the Seattle Center Opera House, the Chicago Auditorium Theatre, the Philadelphia Academy of Music, the Atlanta Fox Theater, the Brooklyn Academy of Music, and the Pasadena Civic Auditorium—in addition, of course, to playing at the Oscar extravaganza at the Shrine Auditorium in Los Angeles.

In Canada, David played at the Theatre St.-Denis in Montreal and at the Roy Thomson Hall in Toronto. He traveled on to Britain in May, giving a concert at the Royal Festival Hall in London; then up to the English Midlands to play at the Royal Centre in Nottingham, back to London to perform at the Theatre Royal in Drury Lane and twice more at the Royal Festival Hall, and then back to the Midlands, playing at the Birmingham Symphony Hall. The tour organizers could hardly have arranged a more punishing timetable.

David returned to the U.S. in August and September and performed at the Los Angeles Hollywood Bowl, San Francisco's Nob Hill Masonic Hall (again), Cleveland's Severance Hall, the Detroit Opera House, and Miami's Dade County Auditorium. In October, David once again crossed the Atlantic to Britain, playing at Glasgow's Royal Concert Hall, in Belfast, and at London's Royal Albert Hall, just a few steps away from the Royal College of Music where he had studied thirty years earlier. By year's end he would have appeared in Europe—in France, Switzerland, Germany, and elsewhere—before flying off to Japan and Southeast Asia, to perform in Seoul, Tokyo, Sendai, Nagoya, Osaka, and Taipei; at the same time plans were already being made for a further international tour of fifty concerts in 1998.

In the entire history of classical music performance, there can hardly have been a wider gap between critical reaction on the one hand and public reaction on the other. While my brother's tour elicited some of the most savage reviews ever bestowed on a classical musician from professional critics, he captivated the general public. Almost all his concerts were sold out well in advance and he received rapturous applause wherever he played. At the first concert in Auckland, New Zealand, the audience of 2,200 rose to their feet to acclaim his performance. The reaction was no less enthusiastic in America. In Boston, a 3,000-strong audience gave him four standing ovations. At the two sellout concerts in Chicago's 110-year-old Auditorium Theatre, all 3,600 seats were filled on both nights. The 150-year-old historic Academy of Music in Philadelphia was surrounded by scalpers who, according to the *Philadelphia Inquirer,* were selling $75 tickets for four times the price. In Atlanta, David

played to 4,000 people. In Toronto, the 2,700-seat
Roy Thomson Hall was sold out on both nights.
David sold out Los Angeles's 3,000-seat Dorothy
Chandler Pavilion (twice), the 2,900-seat Masonic Hall
in San Francisco (all tickets were sold in two hours),
and London's 2,500-seat Royal Festival Hall (three
times). He even played the "Rach 3" at the 18,000-seat
Hollywood Bowl, with the famed 100-piece
Hollywood Bowl Orchestra, an adjunct of the Los
Angeles Philharmonic.

In New York, Jack Kirkman, associate director of
concerts for the Avery Fisher Hall, said that describing Helfgott's concerts as sellouts "is putting it mildly.
I have been here for the last thirty-four years, and I've
never seen anything like it." Tickets for the 2,800-seat
hall went for three times their normal price on the
black market outside. Inside, David received five
standing ovations.

But as the standing ovations got longer and louder,
the attacks by the critics grew more vituperative.
Almost from the first, they were savage. In a scathing
review of his sellout recitals at the Sydney Opera
House, the *Sydney Morning Herald*'s music critic,
Peter McCallum, claimed that David's success was
based partly on "the appeal of the freak show." He
ascribed my brother's popularity to that idiosyncrasy
in human nature that applauds the peculiar while
condescending to it. "Without the frenzied media and
public acclaim which has greeted *Shine,* Helfgott's
disjointed performances would barely merit attention.
[The reality is that] his trademark chatter and wild
gesturing during performances drained the music of
both its balance and its artistry."

American critics were no kinder. "David Helfgott should not have been in the Symphony Hall last night and neither should the rest of us," said Richard Dyer of the *Boston Globe*. In New York, a few nights later, Isaac Stern actually walked out of David's concert.

The *New York Times* tried as best it could to explain the phenomenon of audience adulation: "Mr. Helfgott is not now a great, or even a particularly good, pianist. If the medium for his 'genius' had been chess or mathematics, his shortcomings would probably have become more quickly and indisputably apparent to more people."

The British critics did not restrain themselves. Michael Wright of the London *Sunday Times* wrote: "Occasionally, between chords, Helfgott allows his arms to dangle, while he puffs like a steam train gearing itself up for a particularly steep incline . . . And then there is the singing. Glenn Gould famously sang along to his own performances of Bach, but at least he sang in tune. Helfgott emits a dirgelike wailing noise, a mumbling to the music." Another critic wrote: "He accompanied his playing with sporadic moans, pitched somewhere between a ghostly wail and a low snore." Another said it was "like sitting in someone's living room listening to them practice."

And there was another comparison to Horowitz— but it was a very different one from the positive comparison David had received in Britain three decades earlier. "Helfgott crashes out parallel octaves with an arm speed to equal that of Horowitz—albeit with an occasionally metallic coarseness more reminiscent of Little Richard," wrote one paper.

David's tour promoters hit back hard against the critics' savagery. They said David's detractors were "snobs who suffer from pianist envy" and that they "resented David's popularity and ability to cross over to a new audience." "I'm sure Richard Dyer [of the *Boston Globe*], the acerbic critic who condemned David's performance, has enjoyed his fifteen minutes of fame. David's fame will last a lifetime," said one of David's tour managers. As the *New York Times* put it, "Helfgott spokespeople heaped scorn on the critics, who were, after all, always intent on spoiling a good thing."

Just in case we needed reminding about the link between the film and the concert tour, Scott Hicks weighed in, telling reporters: "I think there are some critics who perhaps act as sort of self-appointed guardians of an elite culture." Geoffrey Rush, obviously feeling the necessity to defend the film's version of the "true David," told one newspaper the critics were "full of bunk."

Of course, the entire tour was a spin-off of *Shine* and some critics spelled this out. Elizabeth Mehren in the *Los Angeles Times* began her article: "He raced onto the stage with no introduction, because after the movie *Shine,* David Helfgott needed none." Writing in the London *Daily Telegraph* under the title "Taking the Shine Off," Geoffrey Norris said: "The audience affection was overwhelming, the ovations tumultuous. But one central question remained unanswered after this deeply flawed recital by the Australian pianist: who is deluding whom? Brutal though it may be to say so, Helfgott would never be able to fill the Festival Hall, or even be invited to do so, on the strength of his musical abilities alone—if it were not for *Shine*."

Norris continued: "It is delusion on everybody's part—Helfgott's, his promoters', the audience's—to imagine that his performance did any service either to him or to the music on his program . . . When, as here, Beethoven's Appassionata Sonata is not so much fractured as crumbled into rubble, you have to admire Helfgott for merely getting through it rather than for asserting any positive interpretative personality." He lamented that "on a concert circuit bristling with fine pianists, any number of young artists with genuine gifts of technical acumen and interpretative insight would have given their eye teeth to receive this sort of exposure."

A few like-minded members of the public praised the critics. "Bravo to the music critics who have the courage to expose the *Shine* recital tour for the cynical exploitation that it is. The critics are doing their job, harsh as they may be," said one letter to the *Los Angeles Times*. But for every "anti-David" letter there were several "pro-David" ones, as debate raged in newspapers the world over. "Sir, What a shame the critics slated the wonderful concerts by pianist David Helfgott," wrote Mrs. Ann V. Schlachter to the London *Times*. "They may not be conventional presentations of the composers' work, but they certainly bring it to the attention of people who would not normally be interested in classical music."

David, who was now being described as "the best-known pianist in the world," was achieving pop star–like status. And he obliged by behaving like one. Newspaper reports said that "During the standing ovations that inevitably greet his performances, Helfgott often leaves the stage, wandering down to the audience to kiss and hug members of the front row." David was even provided with an assistant on the tour whose sole job was to answer his fan mail.

The way in which the tour pitted critics against audiences around the world became the subject of news reports and analysis. Television crews from Britain, Germany, Luxembourg, and other countries buzzed around outside David's New York recitals interviewing concertgoers on the way in. "The Helfgott phenomenon" elicited a piece in the *New York Times* by James R. Oestreich on "the worrisome state of classical music in the United States." He wrote: "Rejoice, the music world is told. Think of all the potential new listeners who are being reached by the film, the concerts, the recordings. It is indeed possible that a Helfgott experience will provide a first, intriguing exposure to classical music for some listeners. As those of us who came to music late can attest, you have to start somewhere. But it would be hopelessly unrealistic to expect great throngs of new listeners to arise from any [of Helfgott's] sensations."

The audience adulation was in part due to the fact that people thought that David, after his mental breakdown and alleged abuse at the hands of my father, was making a comeback. This belief was fed by media reporting of the tour, which usually mentioned *Shine*. For example, the BBC chose, unwittingly, to reproduce totally fictional scenes from the film as part of its reports:

BERYL: You're David Helfgott.

DAVID: That's right, Beryl, that's right, that's right, that's right.

BERYL: But I used to watch you win all those competitions . . . I'm quite a fan. Do you still play?

DAVID: Oh no, I mustn't, I mustn't.

BERYL: You mustn't?

DAVID: I mustn't . . . I mustn't . . .

Certainly the tour was riding on the back of *Shine* as if it were a true story. The official Internet site promoting the tour told us, "*Shine* dramatically depicts the real-life story of Australian genius pianist David Helfgott."

So, cashing in on the film we had not only the concert tour—with its six managers—but also a couple of classical albums and a brace of books, as well as mugs and T-shirts emblazoned with *Shine*. Gillian's book was sold alongside programs for David's concerts, which cost a hefty $15. Promoters dubbed the tour "The Miracle of Love," leaving no one in any doubt whose love they were talking about. *Shine* had turned David into a publicist's dream, and it seemed the exploitative management team was determined to milk every last drop.

David Helfgott Plays Rachmaninov became one of the biggest-selling classical recordings ever. It entered the No. 1 spot on the U.S. *Billboard* classical chart and remained there for many weeks; it also entered the pop chart at one stage. By the time David gave his New York recital in March 1997, he had already sold 200,000 copies in the United States alone. In Australia, it was top of the charts for six months. He was also at No. 1 on the classical charts in many other countries. "Our stocks were obliterated once the film got Oscar nominations," said a spokesperson for Tower Records in London.

Meanwhile, the film's soundtrack, which included some of David's performances, sold 500,000 copies in the United States alone.

David's second CD, *Brilliantissimo,* a disk of his solo performances, went straight in at No. 1 on the British classical charts when it was released in May 1997. Even a rereleased sheet music version of Rachmaninoff's Third Piano Concerto which, in the spirit of *Shine,* was simply called "Rach 3," sold 5,000 copies in Britain within its first month of sale (March 1997), breaking all records for sheet music sales.

David was not only receiving numerous recording contracts, but exciting offers to play at special events were flooding in. The German Recording Industry invited David to attend the Echo Klassik Awards in September 1997 at the Prince Regent Theatre in Munich. In October, he played at the prestigious annual "Piano en Valois" festival in Bordeaux, France. He also had the privilege of playing on Rachmaninoff's original Steinway, at the Rachmaninoff Villa, the composer's house on the shores of Lake Lucerne in Switzerland.

Throughout the sixty-five-concert world tour,

Gillian was keeping a tight hold on the reins. As the London *Daily Telegraph* put it in a news report of May 5, 1997: "At a press conference the pianist played ten minutes of Liszt and was then helped from the stage shaking his head wildly and unwilling or unable to give interviews. Instead, his wife Gillian was very angry on his behalf at the music critics, claiming that they were not taking his performances seriously . . . She has been criticized for trying to cash in on her husband's new fame by agreeing to a grueling world tour." The tour's web site told us that at the various concert locations "Gillian Helfgott was busy signing her book, *Love You to Bits and Pieces,* which has hit the best-seller list in several countries."

But in my eyes, this tour was a case of "Exploit You to Bits and Pieces"; and when newspapers are using phrases like "The David Helfgott Show," I feel I have to respond. Firstly, my brother is not a freak. He is suffering from a mental illness from which he has not recovered; indeed, I am gravely concerned that he is being deliberately deprived of the correct doses of drugs that would help to make him more "normal," in order to maintain his "freak appeal." (According to David's psychiatrist—a friend of Gillian's—David's medication is carefully balanced so as on the one hand not to diminish his creative powers and on the other hand, not to turn him into a complete "zombie.")

Secondly, although I was shocked by the unrestrained viciousness of some of the reviews (in Australia one critic said that the country was known for its unusual creatures—kangaroos, koalas, and so on—and that David fitted into this category), it is cer-

tainly true that David's playing is not nearly as good
as it used to be, which makes me feel very sad. The
truth is that while *Shine*—the fictional story—won
praise, David—the real person—is being shredded by
the critics precisely because this is today's reality. My
brother is being paraded as a modern-day "Elephant
Man" by a well-oiled publicity machine that has
steered everyone away from the truth. To me it is offensive that when television networks film David,
they use close-up shots of him mumbling away to
himself. I feel this is a gross violation of his privacy
and demonstrates a lack of respect for other human
beings.

While in some ways I am happy that audiences
flock to hear David play and that he receives such enthusiastic acclaim, in other ways, it causes me great
distress. I am concerned about the resulting exploitation of his name. On the surface David is obviously
enjoying himself as he basks in audience adulation,
while running around hugging and kissing people.
But I doubt that my mentally ill brother is truly aware
of what is going on. As newspapers informed us, this
was "not your average classical audience." People
were there as much to participate in David's "true
story" as for the quality of his performance. Perhaps
the critic in New Zealand who wrote that he had the
uneasy feeling that he wasn't so much listening to a
piano recital as eavesdropping on someone's therapy
session was painfully right. "Helfgott was truly once a
great pianist. It's so sad to see him exploited this
way," said the London *Sunday Times*.

I wonder whether someone as psychologically vulnerable as David should ever have been put in a po-

sition where he might be exposed to such criticism in
the first place? I am concerned for David's well-being.
To be suddenly paraded in the world's foremost musical venues and to find oneself undertaking an ardu-
ous ten-month tour is a risky business for someone
with his precarious health. Even the fittest of pianists
would find such a workload extremely punishing. A
few of the critics worried about this, too. For example, Stephen Pettitt of the (London) *Financial Times*
called for a stop to "this grotesque circus before any
more damage is done to Helfgott."

For David, a serious musician who has devoted almost his entire life to the piano, to read such terrible
and cruel reviews both of his performance and his
personality must be heart-rending. Indeed, the indig-
nity of being described in such destructive terms
causes pain to myself and the whole Helfgott family.
The prestigious English magazine *The Gramophone*
declined to review David's recording of Rachmaninoff's
Third Piano Concerto because it was so "appalling."
That David's professional reputation is now in tatters
makes me utterly despondent.

The young David was a brilliant musician. It is no
accident that Cyril Smith, his professor at the Royal
College, said in a letter that "his talent amounts to genius." Before he met Gillian, David would never
"dangle his arms" or "puff like a steam train." He
never used to "ramble senselessly" or have "sloppy
and undependable fingerwork." His playing would
never have been described as "an exaggerated clatter" or "a structureless rubble of notes." On the contrary, he performed consistently for decades, and
always received good reviews. It is only because of

Gillian's interviews with the press—in which she repeats stories about locked pianos, institutionalization,
and David's first wife allegedly selling his piano—that
the idea has been created that David didn't perform
for years until he met her, his savior. Even when he
was already under medication, Claire's loving care
helped ensure David's standard of playing was far
higher than it is now. In July 1973, for example, he
received glowing reviews for his "dazzling" performance of Shostakovich with the West Australian
Symphony Orchestra.

In the 1980s, David was still receiving reviews filled
with superlatives. "Excellent," "breathtaking," "astonishing skill," said a 1987 *Music Maker* review. "His talent is unbelievable," wrote *The Australian* in 1987.
But as the years went by and the myths of *Shine* took
hold, the situation deteriorated. If the film had been
honest about David's illness, I don't believe the critics would have savaged him so mercilessly. Horowitz
and Ogden both suffered mental problems and, to
the best of my knowledge, they were never called
"freaks." The music critics, like the film critics, have
been misled.

Some critics were sharp enough to realize this. As
the *New York Times* wrote: "An ideal Hollywood ending it was not . . . The concert tour disproved *Shine*.
David Helfgott did not prove to be the resurrected pianistic genius, however eccentric, portrayed in the
movie and in the surrounding promotional appara-
tus." Said another critic: "The real David Helfgott was
a sad and disturbing figure, far different from the one
portrayed on screen."

One of the very few critics who saw exactly what

was going on and had the courage to say so, was Terry Teachout, the music critic for the New York *Daily News*. In his review he said: "Two centuries ago, nice people went to asylums on Sunday and gawked at the inmates. But times have changed. Today, we let the inmates out of the asylums and encourage them to live 'normal' lives. Some preach strange religions on street corners; others give concerts at Avery Fisher, and nice people pay $50 a head to watch them, and call it progress."

Mr. Teachout expanded on this theme in a much longer piece he wrote for the magazine *Commentary,* in which he made the crucial connection among *Shine,* Gillian, and David's concert tour. He wrote that: "Central to the message of *Shine* [is that] Helfgott, we are to understand, suffers not from a chronic disease of the brain, treatable by drugs, but from a character disorder, caused by his father's abuse and curable through love. Revealingly, it is after he sleeps with his wife for the first time that he is able at long last to play a concert. . . . [In her book] Gillian Helfgott acknowledges implicitly that he is not competent in the legal sense of the word . . . Yet she firmly insists that Helfgott's inability to function as a 'regular member of society' is not an affliction but a choice—though one, it emerges, which she appears to have made on his behalf . . . No one even slightly familiar with the symptoms of schizophrenia could have failed to see that Geoffrey Rush's brilliant performance in *Shine* was—to put it bluntly—a lie. The real David Helfgott, it turned out, still wore the mask of insanity . . . A handful of people in Avery Fisher Hall realized what was happening: a mentally incom-

petent man was being paraded before a paying audience for the financial gain of his managers."

Teachout continues: "Helfgott is mentally ill, and
his physical presence on the stage of a great concert
hall was thus utterly inappropriate. . . . We should be
haunted by the image of that pitiful man at the piano,
whose wife has deliberately chosen to deprive him of
the chance to live as others do. . . . Even now, Gillian
Helfgott can still blandly write in her memoir, 'I will
fight for David's right to stay extraordinary, and do
whatever is necessary to protect him from any pres-
sures to conform.' The more one ponders these self-
righteous words, the clearer it becomes that to speak
of the marketing of David Helfgott as an act of exploitation is to use too weak a word. It is, rather, a
sin."

20

DAVID AND GILLIAN

In the wake of the media blitz surrounding *Shine* and David's concert tour, the world now associates my brother with strange physical behavior and his "trademark babble." On television, David's newly developed habits are there for all to see, as he fidgets and chatters nervously, keeping his eyes half shut, or eagerly clutches and gropes at people all around him. It is now clear that David has not been "nurtured to recovery," as one might expect from the publicity surrounding *Shine*. On the contrary, his speech has deteriorated to that of a child. David, who turned fifty in 1997, repeats words frenetically—"It's great. It's awesome. It's great. It's awesome"—and chuckles oddly at words that only he finds amusing, such as "fun pun, what a game."

One of the habits David has adopted is to pepper his sentences in a rather pretentious way with French words. He'll describe something as *"joyeux"* rather than "joyous." He'll talk about placing his *"couteau"* (knife) on his *"assiette"* (plate). And he'll say *"parce que"* instead of "because" in the middle of an otherwise English sentence. He also likes to use words from Polish, Russian, Italian, and Yiddish, or to make up words altogether, such as "dentifies" (teeth), "greedos" (greedy), "matinata" (morning), "lazos" (lazy), and "wishywashy" (dirty laundry). David even jokes around about his beloved composers. He'll casually refer to "Tchaik" (Tchaikovsky); the "Rach 3" is now "a whopper"; of Ravel, he'll say, laughing to himself like a little boy: "Poor old Maurice, he might unravel." As Geoffrey Rush told the London *Sunday Times:* "Scott Hicks gave me hours of tapes of interviews with David, and I used them as a kind of Berlitz 'How to Speak Fluent David Helfgott.'"

The physical side to David's behavior is also rather embarrassing. He smothers practically everyone within reach with kisses on their cheeks and foreheads. Often he misses the mark, but when he does hit the target, he mocks himself, saying: "That was a good one." He goes up to virtual strangers and calls them "darling," before furiously hugging or petting them.

While some people find this side of David's personality utterly endearing, for me it is the cause of great anguish. His speech and behavior belie the great intellectual faculties my brother possesses. David remains perfectly capable of holding normal conversations on complex subjects. Last time we met, he wanted to discuss the way coalition governments are formed in Israel and the latest developments in the NASA space exploration program. Psychiatrists say that this kind of paradoxical situation, where a person displays both considerable intellectual powers and jittery, high-speed incoherent speech patterns replete with rambling word associations, is common with an illness such as David's.

But while the primary reason for his abnormal behavior is his illness, I believe that the marked downward turn in his condition of recent years has been exacerbated by outside factors. These strange, negative changes in his behavior and speech really only began to manifest themselves after he married Gillian in August 1984, gaining ground gradually, as I explained in Chapter 14. Before he met Gillian, he would occasionally murmur, sigh, or rock his piano stool to the music, but he never interrupted the fluidity of his playing. He never approached hotel porters and babbled in their ear or hugged passersby in the street. He didn't stoop and shuffle the way he does now, or call musical compositions "composodilies."

David used to write to me regularly before he married Gillian, and these letters were articulate, interesting, and lively. But since they married, Gillian has done all the letter-writing herself, allowing David to only sign his name and add kisses and occasionally a few words at the bottom.

One of the most marked changes has occurred in the way David talks about his family. Before he came under Gillian's influence, David said only positive things. For example, he told one Australian newspaper that "Les has been a tremendous brother to me through both the good and bad years." But now David is "quoted" in Gillian's book as calling Leslie

"Barmy on the Army," something that neither Leslie nor anybody else has ever heard him say, and which Leslie is quite upset by.

David used to tell everybody how much he loved his family and how much he had missed us when he was in London. For example, he told *The West Australian* (December 17, 1983): "I missed my family [in London]" and he told *The National Times* (January 6, 1984) that his breakdown in London was due to "the lack of a family life in the big city . . . I missed my family." In marked contrast, in 1995 he told his biographer Beverley Eley: "For twenty-five years [until I met Gillian in 1983] no one really gave a damn whether I lived or died. It was a long, long time in the wilderness." "Twenty-five years" takes us back to 1958, when David was eleven, and is an insult not just to my father, mother, myself, and my siblings, but also to Frank Arndt, Madame Carrard, Claire, the Harrises, the Prices, Dot, the Reverend Fairman, and many others. I simply do not believe these sentiments represent David's own thoughts.

But they do sound very similar to what Gillian relates in her book, *Love You to Bits and Pieces:* "By marrying David, I would not only confirm his trust in my commitment to him [but] make a gesture of validating him as an individual wholly accepted and loved by at least one person on the planet."

It doesn't surprise me that the most hostile statements attributed to David in Gillian's book are directed against Gillian's two main rivals for love in David's life: Claire and my father. Claire is described as a "bitch." As for my father, Gillian quotes David saying: "Father's just a hypocrite, he's two-faced" and

"Daddy didn't have any contacts, he didn't have any money, he never had any money! But me, I've got money! I've got money!" He also talks of "Dad's cruelty" and "rich Jews," phrases none of us had heard from him before Gillian came on the scene.

Some of the other things David has said about Dad in public are just vile. "My father castrated me," he announced to one gathering. Often, he'll say something that is exactly the opposite of the truth. He'll say: "Daddy wouldn't let me play tennis! *Quelle dommage!* [What a pity]," when in fact the whole family can confirm that it was Dad who encouraged David to play tennis and David who wasn't interested. (Of course David never says anything horrible like this when he is speaking to me or his family.)

These words do actually come out of my brother's mouth, but it seems that he may just be "following orders." At a concert in Perth in 1997 David announced that "Daddy was a bastard." A shocked Leslie and Marie, who happened to be there, went up to David and asked him why he said such a thing. He whispered to Leslie: "Because Gillian says so."

It now also seems that David is forbidden from saying nice things about his family in public. When interviewed on *The South Bank Show* on British television on June 22, 1997, he told the presenter, Melvyn Bragg: "Margaret supports me. She came all the way from Israel to see me last year," and then he lowered his voice a little and said: "but Gillian doesn't like me to say that."

On the same program, after David said: "Daddy was cruel, Daddy was cruel," Melvyn Bragg asked him: "But how was your daddy cruel, David?" David was at a loss for words. He couldn't answer him, because he knew in his heart that there was no truth in what he was saying.

This denigration of my father and of the family as a whole coincides with Gillian's own spectacular self-promotion. From 1986 onward, article after article stated that it was she alone "who restored his health." At the same time, David's reputation was being hyped up. One article in Australia even said that not just Isaac Stern but Daniel Barenboim, too, had hailed him as a genius. At the same time, Gillian became rather elusive about what was actually wrong with David. In a piece about Gillian and David entitled "Cultivating a genius" in the May 24, 1986 edition of the *Western Mail* magazine, it was reported that "Gillian won't let reporters pry into the cause of her husband's mental breakdown. 'It's too complex to explain in an article without hurting people, but they were personal problems rather than professional problems,' she said, denying that the pressure of his London studies caused the problem." In direct contradiction to his doctors' reports, Gillian declared that David's "health was not too good" during the period he was living at the lodge.

In her book, instead of giving credit to all the efforts his family have made for David over the years, Gillian lavishes praise on people whom I have never heard of before. For example, she devotes several pages to someone called Nils Ruben, who Gillian claims did a great deal for David's career all over Denmark, and provided "precisely the type of musical interaction which David had been longing for in

Australia and which was so difficult to secure for him there."

Gillian is attempting to ensure that David remains distanced from his family even in the event of her death. I am told that in her will, she has left half of what she owns to David but it will be held in a trust to be administered by her children from her first marriage. In other words, in the event that she dies first, her children will have more say in my brother's life than his own flesh and blood.

Above all, *Shine* portrays Gillian in an extremely positive light. When she met Scott Hicks, Gillian was already familiar with the world of film. Her first husband, John Murray, is a film producer, her son Scott is a film director and her daughter, Sue, is Director of Marketing for the Australian Film Commission. Hicks should surely have known better than to rely so heavily on Gillian, who provided a version of events so utterly geared to promoting herself. Hicks's other main source was David, who admits that as far as his past is concerned he has what he refers to as a "fog in his head."

In various interviews David has said: "It's only a game, mostly a game; a great game, if you don't weaken"; and: "I reckon it's a game, darling?"; and "You can do anything you like, is that right, darling? Up to a point, up to pun fun!" If this is a game, it's not a very funny one. Hicks should have checked out what David refers to as his "game" with others before making a film and passing it off as a true version of events.

I am convinced that David's game playing is motivated not by malice or cunning, but rather by his illness. When I compare his condition during the period that the Reverend Fairman was supervising his medication to the way he is now, I wonder whether he is receiving as effective a treatment as he was then. As I mentioned in the last chapter, I am very concerned that—to quote *Newsweek* (March 10, 1997)— "his meds [medications] are calibrated to keep him zippy enough to play." In an extensive interview with Gillian in the (London) *Daily Mail,* Jane Kelly writes about Gillian: "She had to take him [David] over. She cut him off from his friends and family. All this was necessary to put him back on the road to performing. It was a hard slog. Gillian gradually reduced his level of drugs. . . . 'I've had to be firm with him and I've had to have control over him. But it has all been worth it,' she said. When she met him, he was thin, penniless . . . Now he is healthy, celebrated." Although it is an appalling concept, it can't be ruled out that his medication is being deliberately adjusted so as to maintain his appeal as an eccentric.

Indeed, on ABC television's "Nightline Friday Night Special" entitled *Encore,* and broadcast just before the Oscars, Gillian refers to David's medication and says: "David could be somewhat different to what he is if his medication was increased, but then what is the outcome of increasing the medication? I could be robbing him of his ecstasy, of his fantasy, of his journey into his musical world. He would perhaps be less exhausting in some ways to live with, but at what cost?"

There is no cure yet for schizophrenia, but antipsychotic medication can now greatly help in controlling many of its symptoms. Studies show that

about one-third of those with schizophrenia or schizophrenia-related illnesses suffer from delusions and
feelings of paranoia, often directed against a family
member. But as three leading experts, John Thornton,
Mary Seeman, and Elizabeth Plummer, of the Clarke
Institute of Psychiatry at the University of Toronto,
have stressed: "Delusional statements should be
heard, considered and rejected firmly and without
emotion." Gillian appears to be doing exactly the opposite.

I believe that the horrible, untrue things that David
has started saying in recent years not only hurt and
defame others, but also have an unhealthy effect on
David himself. I believe that on a deeper level, he
cannot feel at peace about what he is saying; this is
not the real David. During our family reunion in Perth
in August 1996, Suzie threw a party at her home to
celebrate Louise's birthday, and Gillian and David
came. We all had a lot of fun, playing the piano,
singing, and laughing. Everyone avoided mentioning
Shine. At one stage I said to David, "You have done
very well, David. Dad would be very proud of you."
And David said to me, "Oh Dad, Dad, yes he would
have been so proud of me." Tears came to his eyes.
I could see he was very moved by that thought.

Being placed in a defenseless position, in which he
has almost no choice other than to utter misleading
and untrue statements in order to please others, must
have a debilitating effect on his health. I honestly believe that if David were to utter the truthful words
"Daddy was kind, Daddy was good" (which he
knows in his soul and heart to be the case), then not
only his medical state but also his piano playing

would benefit enormously. Saying things that he doesn't really mean creates a dichotomy inside his psyche, which damages him generally, and makes his playing so fragmented.

It is my firm belief that in spite of the negative statements about my father that have been attributed to him in the press, my brother loves my father now as he always has done. I love David dearly. He is sweet-natured, generous, and courageous and I do not believe he really knows or means what he says.

21

A SMALL VICTORY KEEPS THE *SHINE STUDY GUIDE* OUT OF AUSTRALIAN SCHOOLS

Late one evening in December 1996, my brother Leslie called me in a panic from Perth. He had discovered that the Australian Teachers of Media (ATOM) had prepared a *Shine Study Guide* on behalf of Ronin Films, *Shine's* film distribution company in Australia.

Ronin Films had already started sending the guide to Australian high schools. It consists of a video of the film, the screenplay, a copy of Gillian's book *Love You to Bits and Pieces,* and detailed study sheets for teachers and pupils. There are questions for children to work on and "issues" for class discussion. Individual sheets have headings such as "Personal Development and Health," "Studies of Society and Environment," and "Psychology." The guide was destined for students of English, health and human relations, psychology, sociology, media studies, music and the arts.

When Leslie obtained a copy and saw what it contained, he was aghast. It was bad enough that the guide included *Love You to Bits and Pieces,* but when he read what was written on the study sheets, he was on the verge of tears. It was the realization of our worst nightmare.

The *Shine Study Guide* announces that "*Shine* explores moral and psychological issues," and the discussion questions imply that the characters in the film directly correspond to the real-life ones. The idea that generations of school children were going to be encouraged to answer questions, write synopses, and then hold class discussions on my father's alleged behavior was abhorrent. Questions include "Are the other children subject to Peter's strict control?" Children are asked to "make a list of words and phrases to describe David's father," and to discuss "David's banishment from home" and how Gillian brought "stability and love into David's chaotic life . . . [which] helped him to come to terms with . . . his father and resolve the traumas of the past." Some statements contain completely unwarranted assertions. The "Society and Environment" section begins: "Peter seems to want to punish David for the fact that he hasn't suffered in his life . . . *Shine* shows us how one individual's world breaks down when he comes into conflict with his own father . . . Brainstorm some of these points in group discussion and share your point of view." It then instructs pupils to "consider the differences in the attitudes of Peter and Ben Rosen toward religion."

Under the heading "Family Values" is the statement: "Peter was a Polish Jew; he and David's mother had reared their children in poverty, but maintained a rigorous set of values." Points for discussion are then listed. "Was the family destroyed by David's departure?" is one.

The "Psychological Breakdown" section fails to mention mental illness at all or to say that David has a recognized psychotic condition. Instead, in the style of Gillian and Scott Hicks's press conferences and media interviews, the guide repeatedly uses the word "eccentric" to describe my brother. It also talks about his "recovery."

The "Psychology" section encourages discussion of "Freudian developmental theory." It states: "This film is a tragic story of a father-son relationship . . . David and his family were under the influence of a very dominant, authoritarian father . . . yet it shows us how an indomitable spirit may recover from even the most devastating of psychological setbacks." There are questions on "authoritarian parenting styles." "Make sure you are familiar with the characteristics of the stages of alarm, resistance, and exhaustion," exhorts the guide.

In the "Personal Development" section is the statement: "In David's earlier childhood he is clearly controlled by his father." The guide asks why Peter was "so obsessed about winning?" Students are asked to "write or orally present a character profile of Peter." Katherine Pritchard's quasimother role in the film does not go unremarked. Questions for the students include: "What part does the character Katherine play in David's life? Why does Peter decide that Katherine is not acceptable?"

The *Shine Study Guide* even includes a paragraph about the symbolic use of water in the film—including "David's tears," "the menace of a dripping bath tap before David's father hit him," and how David is "head above water" when he finds sanctuary in Gillian's swimming pool.

I found the entire guide extremely upsetting, and some parts of it actually made me feel nauseous. Children are asked to discuss the statement: "David's return to performance is made possible by the love and encouragement of Gillian, Sylvia, and *HER* family who nurtured David, believe in him, and tolerate his eccentricity." In the "Musical Perspective" section, students are directed to "the magically evocative scene that pans from [Peter's] grave to an entire cemetery accompanied by Vivaldi's soaring 'Nulla In Mundo Pax Sincera' . . . [which] becomes David and Gillian's theme." It then asks: "Why is it such an appropriate piece of music for the final scene?"

As if *Shine* hadn't caused us enough distress, we now had to live with the knowledge that high school children throughout Australia would be analyzing our family in detail and scrutinizing our early lives. For Leslie, the idea that his children would be reading this entirely fictionalized view of their grandfather in class and then discussing it with their classmates was just too much. My mother and sisters were equally outraged that my other nieces and nephews would be receiving these supposed insights into their "brutal" grandfather as part of their education.

Leslie's wife Marie had already told me that their little daughter Dorothy had been asking her mom: "I don't understand. You promise me that Grandpa wasn't such a bad man, so why do they show him like that in the film if it's not true?" Imagine how their young son, Peter, named after his grandfather, was going to feel.

The use of study guides and "teaching through film" has become widespread in recent years. Such guides include those for Kenneth Branagh's *Hamlet, Twelfth Night, Gorillas in the Mist,* and *Gulliver's Travels*. If this is the only way in today's television age of encouraging students to familiarize themselves with otherwise difficult classics, so be it. But to the best of my knowledge, the study guide for *Shine* is unique in that it is the only one accompanying a film passing itself off as fact when it is nothing of the sort. None of the other guides submitted as part of the school curriculum use real people with their real names, most of whom are still alive.

No one had bothered to inform us, let alone ask our permission about what can only be described as a gross violation of the Helfgott family's privacy, going beyond all bounds of sensitivity and decency.

Research by marketing companies indicates that guides are more likely to be used if sent to teachers directly, thus bypassing the school bureaucracy. Some packs had already been sent to schools, but widespread distribution throughout Australia was due to begin in early 1997. Realizing that there was no time to waste, Leslie, aided by his wife, leaped into action. He immediately called Andrew Pike of Ronin Films, and pleaded with him to withdraw the *Shine Study Guide* from schools. He explained to Pike everything that was wrong with *Shine* and why the Helfgott family found it so offensive. Shocked at what he heard, Pike was sympathetic to our plight from the very beginning. He said he would look into the problem and see if it could be resolved.

Leslie then contacted ATOM, but was told they couldn't—or wouldn't—do anything to stop the study kit going to schools. In desperation, he next turned to the superintendent of the Education Department, but was told that they, too, were unable to stop the study guide's distribution.

Leslie and Marie, who were spending sleepless nights worrying about what could be done, then contacted Barbara Hocking of SANE (the Schizophrenia Australia Foundation). "We were amazed that such a study guide concerning a well-known mentally ill person was being distributed without professional review and approval by SANE or a similar mental health organization," Barbara told me on the telephone a short while later. "We were concerned that while there was much discussion about parenting styles, with the clear implication that these were the cause of David's 'psychological setback,' there was no mention that David has schizo-affective disorder. A whole generation of school students were to be misinformed about the causes of psychotic illness."

Hocking contacted Ronin Films and told them in no uncertain terms that all SANE's work would go to waste if inaccurate information about mental illness was issued to school children ignorant of the issues.

Leslie and Marie's task was not confined to Australia. We heard that the *Shine Study Guide* was to be distributed in other countries, too. Margaret Leggatt, president of the World Schizophrenia Fellowship, who lives in Australia, wrote to the National Alliance for the Mentally Ill (NAMI), in

Arlington, Virginia, and to schizophrenia support groups in Canada and England, saying that she was gravely concerned that "the guide for school students . . . perpetuates the idea of the father's brutality causing the schizo-affective breakdown." Dr. Fuller Torrey of NAMI, author of *Surviving Schizophrenia: A Family Manual,* replied that they would do "whatever we can to correct the grossly mistaken etiological implications of *Shine.*"

In January, there was the first sign that the campaign was making some headway. Andrew Pike told Leslie that he had read Gillian's book and that it would be removed from the study guide. The other materials, however, would remain.

Leslie and Marie intensified their efforts, managing to speak to a member of parliament about their anxieties. Meanwhile, SANE prepared a special flier for insertion into the *Shine Study Guide,* giving factual explanations about the nature and causes of mental illness. They attempted to get hold of a list of schools that had already received copies of the guide, in order to send them the fliers and counteract the damage done.

Throughout this time, SANE not only did valuable work but, in marked contrast to the makers of *Shine,* they kept in constant touch with the Helfgott family, including myself, keeping us informed of any developments and offering reassuring and sympathetic words. These were of great comfort. At that time we really felt that it was us against the world: the film industry, the media, and the publishing industry.

On May 15, 1997, Andrew Pike wrote to Leslie, saying that the flier prepared by SANE would be incorporated in the guides and that a prominent disclaimer sticker would be placed on the front of the guide; this would point out that the guide was not meant to relate to real persons or actual events. He also told Leslie how much he regretted the fact that a disclaimer had not been put at the beginning of the film.

Although we were obviously happy that some progress had been made, we were still far from satisfied. If there had been a prominent disclaimer at the start of the film, the whole audience would have had the opportunity to read it; teachers and school children may well look at individual sheets and components of the guide, however, without properly registering the statement on the cover. Our real names were still being used in the guide, and this, together with the influence of the film itself and all the surrounding publicity, made us fear that children would still be left with the impression that the events were true. At the very least, Leslie wanted a disclaimer on every individual sheet clearly stating that *Shine* was a work of fiction and that the family portrayed in the film bore no resemblance to the real Helfgott family. "For God's sake, have some compassion," he told Pike. "My mother's still alive."

Leslie and Marie didn't let up, and their valiant and determined efforts finally paid off. Despite the fact that his business was distribution, Andrew Pike came to the conclusion that the privacy of our family was being violated in a completely unacceptable way. When he phoned Leslie in early June to tell him that the guide would be withdrawn, the whole family was overjoyed. Pike said Ronin Films would also try to recall the guides from the more than 1,000 schools that had already received them. He confirmed Ronin Films's abandonment of the *Shine Study Guide* by letter to Leslie on June 16, 1997. Although it wasn't made clear exactly what had changed his mind, we were all immensely relieved.

Unfortunately, as I write, the *Shine Study Guide* is still available elsewhere in the world. An article in the *New York Times* confirmed that in the United States, *Shine Study Guide*s had already been sent to "teachers of music, psychology, sociology and history." Vincent Nebrida, senior manager for marketing and special projects at Fine Line Features, *Shine*'s U.S. distributors, was quoted as saying that history teachers were included on the distribution list because "*Shine* touches on the whole Holocaust aspect."

In addition to normal distribution channels, we also have today's new technologies to contend with when trying to prevent the guide's dispersal. The guide is also available for downloading free of charge on the Internet from the Fine Line Features web site. ". . . Nor did it stop with the movie," it says on the web site. "Download the free *Shine Study Guide*! Lifetime Learning Systems, in cooperation with Momentum Films and Fine Line Features, has created a special educational study guide based on *Shine*, titled *Shine: The Triumph of Self-Expression*. This educational program—designed for older high school students and college students—builds upon the many themes explored in the film, including the development of human personality, family dynamics, and the music in the film. Although the material is copyrighted, you have permission to photocopy as many sets of the study guide as you may need for educational purposes."

(Regrettably, there is also a "student study assignment" on the Internet for *"Love You to Bits and Pieces,"* full of nonsense about "the psychological illnesses that can come from playing the piano," and statements such as *"Shine* took a lot of effort to make everything as accurate as possible.")

As I write this, I am still unsure what the future position will be regarding the *Shine Study Guides* in America and other countries, but at least we now know that Peter Helfgott's six grandchildren won't have to sit in class in Australia and hear teachers and fellow students discuss their grandfather and all the lies concocted about him by Scott Hicks's film.

22

RIGHTING THE WRONGS

Anyone living in western society knows that the film industry and the media are extremely powerful. However, until you've experienced their full weight at firsthand, it is difficult to appreciate just how much influence they wield. At times during the struggle to present the truth over *Shine,* we felt that we were battling against the whole world. When an Oscar-winning film, backed by a massive publicity and marketing operation, feeds myths to an eager media, it is almost impossible for private individuals with limited resources to set the record straight. Once the "story" is picked up you feel as ineffective as a Lilliputian in the land of the giants, a tiny voice drowned out by the surrounding clamor.

Scott Hicks is well aware of the overwhelming force of the media. This is why I find it so reprehensible that, not content with the damage done by his film, he has decided to continue hurting the Helfgott family and perpetrating his fraud on an unsuspecting public by making use of newspapers and television. It is no coincidence that time and again *Shine* is called a "true story" in media around the world. Hicks does everything he can to suggest it is. He adds insult to injury by repeatedly telling journalists that he has been sensitive to the feelings of the Helfgott family. He called a pre-Oscar press conference in Los Angeles to inform the *New York Times* and other major newspapers and TV networks that in his "ten-year odyssey" to make *Shine,* he had undertaken "meticulous research" to ensure that "everything in the film" was based on fact. And, as if to demonstrate that he had the full support of the Helfgott family, Gillian (but not David) stood resolutely by his side.

Hicks's claim that his film was based on testimony "not just from David's memory but from the people who knew him" is patent nonsense. Tom Gross and I did not have ten years to research and write this book. We had only a few weeks. Yet in that time we managed to speak to almost all the key players in David's life. We found that Hicks had talked to almost none of them. They were all readily available and easy to track down. All had clear memories of David that they were more than willing to share with us; they were, without exception, surprised, angered, and upset by the way *Shine* had misled the public.

After twenty-one chapters in which I have, as best I could, tried to right the wrongs shown in his film, I would like to ask some questions of Hicks. Why did he feel it necessary, after referring to David as "a stray dog" in the film, to further defame people with whom he hasn't even had the courtesy to speak, by telling a large gathering of journalists that David was "lying and dying on the floor" before he met Gillian? Why did he deny the existence of David's first wife, Claire, who did so much for David? Why doesn't his film pay tribute to the Reverend Robert Fairman, who has received parliamentary citations for his tireless work for the mentally ill and the excellent standards he has maintained at his lodges? Why did he not show David's close friend of eight years, Dot, taking David to concerts, as she often did?

Scott Hicks should ask himself how it is possible for an acclaimed film director to make a movie about a real human being without speaking to most of the key players in his life. How is it that most of the film focuses on David as a music student and yet neither of David's main music teachers, Frank Arndt and Madame Carrard, were consulted? Or Professor Sir Frank Callaway, a highly respected figure in classical music circles around the world, who could have told Hicks that Peter Helfgott had not opposed David's going to London? What about Phyllis Sellick or Professor Immelman, who were present during David's 1969 London performance of Rachmaninoff's Third Piano Concerto? Or Sir Keith Falkner, director of the Royal College of Music, who could have related how David described his Pop as "a super human being"?

If his film is "rooted clearly in fact" and "paints a very honest picture of David," as Hicks has told journalists, then why not mention the history of mental illness in the Helfgott family? Why conceal the fact that David played the "Rach 3" many times before he left for London and gave other triumphant performances after his return? Why not make clear that David was being cared for at home by my father until his death in 1975? Why discard David's tribute to Dad in the newspaper after he died? Why not confirm with Isaac Stern his offer of bringing David to America? Wouldn't it have been a courtesy if Hicks had found a few minutes during the ten years he took to make *Shine* to speak to Phyllis Sellick before presenting her internationally renowned husband as a doddery old fool who says you have to be "mad" to attempt the "Rach 3"?

Apart from recognizing that he has caused the Helfgott family and our friends incalculable distress, I feel that Hicks should think long and hard about the fact that psychiatrists and medical organizations in at least three continents have had to divert their time from their valuable work with the mentally ill to take a public stand against what is after all a mere movie. He should also think long and hard about why many people find his treatment of Jews and Judaism, and of Holocaust survivors in particular, deeply offensive.

If Hicks had been the slightest bit interested in telling a true story he would have spoken to myself, my mother, and Leslie; he would have been fascinated by all the wonderful letters we have that my father and David exchanged, which show their warmth and affection for each other and the vitality of the atmosphere in our house. But, of course, Hicks wasn't interested. He seems to have taken rather too seriously Sam Goldwyn's quip: "My mind is made up! Don't confuse me with the facts!"

If his motives in making this film were purely artistic, if he was merely interested in the story line he had created, rather than playing around with the lives of the Helfgott family, he could have made virtually the same film simply by using fictional names and changing a few details. This would not have affected its impact as a work of art. The story would still have been powerful and imaginative, with a villain for the audience to boo and a heroine to save the day. But Hicks rejected this option, and it is clear that his motives were not purely artistic. He was determined to abuse the truth and use the real David Helfgott for commercial exploitation.

Hicks has admitted his film is not true, which is why his disclaimer reads: "While the characters David and Gillian Helfgott are actual persons, this film also depicts characters and events which are fictional, which do not and are not intended to refer to any real person or any actual event." But Hicks wants it both ways. He knows that if people believe *Shine* to be true, it will be a more gripping film, bring in larger financial rewards, and win greater critical acclaim. Consequently he made the disclaimer so small and obscure as to render it virtually meaningless, thereby deceiving the public and the media alike. And to ensure that everything goes to plan, he has continued to feed the media his myths about "meticulous research" and so on, many months after the film's release.

It is no accident that so many people were taken in by *Shine* and found its myths so acceptable. It's not just on account of the fact that it is technically a well-made film, with some very strong performances and a slick publicity machine behind it. It is because Hicks imbued his film with elements that he knew would have widespread appeal to many people, themes that tugged at heartstrings, stirred emotions, and confirmed preexisting myths—a wicked father and a wonderful woman as redeemer; child abuse; a triumph over mental illness. He also exploited the well-known psychological phenomenon of "blaming the victim"—which when the victim is a concentration camp survivor is almost bound to bring unconscious anti-Semitism into play.

Mix all these together and you have a surefire winner. Who can resist such "a joyous celebration," as the (London) *Daily Telegraph* put it, "of the triumph of good over evil, genius over madness, light over darkness . . . in the form of the radiant astrologer Gillian, who rescues David from the edge of madness, and brings the film to the happiest of conclusions?" Once the media started, there was no stopping them.

And for the finale of our "true story" let's produce the real David Helfgott—on Oscar night no less—although we had better tell everyone he's only an eccentric and has made a complete recovery from his mysterious illness, otherwise people might suspect that this poor man is still mentally ill and unaware of the way he is being exploited by the circus all around him. The world fell in love with David's tale. Only David is not Forrest Gump. He is a real person.

The problem with the impact of *Shine* and the damage and hurt it has caused myself and my family is a circular one. It is precisely because people believe the film to be true that it is such a moving and gripping piece of cinema. And the more moving and gripping it is, the greater the damage it does.

For the Helfgott family to succeed in counteracting

the media blitz that followed *Shine* was virtually impossible. It was made even harder by the existence of the new electronic media, which enables anyone with access to a computer to reach a worldwide audience. As I sat at home in Beersheva on Oscar night, I asked myself whether it was a coincidence that *Shine*'s official Internet site states that "when David returns to Australia . . . his father behaves as if his son is dead"—almost the exact same words Billy Crystal used in front of one billion people watching the Oscars.

What my family has gone through is not an experience I would wish on anyone. Hicks seems to be remarkably pleased with the success his film has brought him. "If it was possible to be killed with praise, I would be long dead," he told one interviewer modestly. He doesn't realize and simply doesn't care what a wonderful man Peter Helfgott was. I doubt whether Hicks knows how many people he has upset by catapulting my father to worldwide infamy. Dr. Jack Morris, a close friend of my father's, exclaimed: "How dare anyone speak about Peter Helfgott like that? He was one of the greatest men I ever met"; Mrs. Miriam Lemish, who was a bridesmaid at my parents' wedding, told me she cried after she left the theater; Sam Kras described Peter as a "happy, genial man, a real character, and extremely likable"; Ida Zoltak called Peter "a gentle and lovable man"; Ivan Rostkier described *Shine* as "a shocking film. Peter was a man with such a good heart, and so wonderful to talk to because he knew so much"; Gertie Granek said: "What a father he was. They should have given him a medal." These are the people who actually knew my father. But Hicks and Gillian, two people who never met him, seem quite happy to trample on his good name and reap the profits.

There is another victim here: David. Even though on the face of it *Shine* is sympathetic to him, depicting him as both a hero and a victim, I believe that in fact it humiliates him. David's life is held up to public viewing in the most distasteful way. He is shown defecating in the bathtub, walking around with his penis dangling in front of his landlady in London, grabbing the breasts of strange women, bouncing naked on a trampoline, dumping sheet music in the swimming pool, and so on. Hicks asks the audience to view these things not as troubling but as cute. Yet it exposes my brother to ridicule, and in effect belittles him. The reality is that mental illness is neither quaint, lovable, nor amusing. Certainly not to those who suffer from it and not to their loved ones who care for them.

Much as Hicks and Gillian would like to convince themselves that David is merely some kind of free-spirited eccentric, a cuddly, creative oddball with extremely erratic behavior—he is not. He suffers from a serious mental illness, which raises questions about how far he was able to give informed consent to the making of *Shine*. It is doubtful whether he is capable of objectively judging the impact of such a controversial film or the way it has infringed his own right to privacy.

The nightmare has been going for a long time now, but I still live in hope that one of these days Scott Hicks might be brave enough to do the right thing. If only he would stop telling journalists about his "meticulous research," apologize to me and my family, insert a disclaimer at the start of videos of *Shine* and at the beginning of the published screenplay, and completely withdraw *Shine Study Guide*s from schools worldwide. We can only hope.

It has been a great struggle for me to clear my father's name. Once the media latch onto a myth that appeals to the public, the protests of private individuals are liable to get completely swamped. By writing this book, I have done my best to make the truth known, but I realize that there's little chance of ever really repairing the damage to my father's reputation. It will be some compensation, though, if others in the movie and publishing industries take the lesson of *Shine* to heart; if they learn to check their facts more carefully and become more aware of the suffering they can inflict on innocent people if they don't.

As I write, *Shine* continues to be described in many of the world's newspapers and on television networks as "the ultimate feel-good film," "a happily-ever-after tale" and the "feel-good story that is so totally uplifting because it's true." Filmgoers may leave the theater moved and uplifted, but for the Helfgott family, there has been no happy ending.

INDEX